God's Good Earth

An Environmental Bible Study

By Debbie McGuire

<u>Dedication</u>

For Mike, Svenja and Erin:
My hope is that you will inherit a healthy environment.

For my husband, Paul,
who unknowingly married a conservationist,
but who faithfully goes along
with my lifestyle.

Contents

Introduction

2 Samuel 23:4 (NIV)
He is like the light of morning at sunrise on a cloudless morning,
like the brightness after rain that brings grass from the earth.

Psalm 23:1-3 (ESV)
The Lord is my shepherd; I shall not want. He makes me lie down in green pastures.
He leads me beside still waters. He restores my soul.

Those who dwell among the beauties and mysteries of the earth
are never alone or weary of life.
By Rachel Carson

If you want to be rejuvenated, energized go outdoors! Find a park, a natural setting complete with blue sky, trees, birds, and spend a bit of time there. I always feel better if I can take a break in such an area. In fact, I would always choose to exercise outdoors over using my exercise bike indoors. So, why is it that being outdoors can rejuvenate us? I believe that it is a way to connect with God's plan for us. Being outdoors in nature gives a view of God's design.

Even though I am not a scientist, I am extremely impressed with God's creation. It is really amazing how all aspects were designed to support human life. These aspects have been analyzed by scientists for thousands of years in order to "figure out how God did it." For example, botanists know how plants absorb sunlight, water and carbon dioxide to grow and to produce fruit, plus how they replicate themselves through seeds. In their photosynthesis process plants absorb carbon dioxide, then, release oxygen as the by-product. Man does the opposite: breathes in oxygen, then, breathes out carbon dioxide. God designed so much of nature in cycles. I would go as far to say that God created the earth like a giant puzzle with all of the pieces fitting precisely together!

I was always inquisitive about the earth's environment, yet in writing this book I have learned about many more complexities of God's creation. My greatest concern is how the balance of God's design has been impacted by the brainwork of man. True, God designed man with a brain and "free choice," but did He want man to change His brilliant design?

God created the earth for human beings. We acknowledge the beauty and intricacy of His creation. The book of Genesis details God's directions to man: to have dominion over the earth, and to be fruitful and multiply. If God commanded humans in this manner, then why do we need to think about "climate change" or "our carbon footprint?" If our natural world is changing in ways that will affect humans' ability to live, then maybe that is what God wanted. Maybe the destruction of the earth is simply what was prophesied in Revelations.

Religious teachings present God as "omniscient," meaning all knowing.   At the same time, teachings allow man "free will" to make his own choices. Putting those ideas together: God knows in advance what choices we will make: good or bad. God already knows about the end of humans on the earth, which will happen through the choices He knew we would make. He already knows how long our earth will be able to sustain us with air, water and food. Plus, He already knows whether we will restrict pollution in order to produce healthy food and water, whether we will limit emissions of greenhouse gases to reduce the warming of our atmosphere, etc.   So, humans will continue to make the choices that God knows they will make. They can choose to take care of the earth, or not.

We can make choices to make our lives and the lives of our children healthier and smoother. Since we do not know how many generations will follow us, consider just your children and grandchildren. How do you want their lives to be? Do you want them to have to move to the mountains after being inundated by coastal flooding?   Do you want them to have to move to northern areas to avoid excessive heat waves? Or, do you want them to be able to eat only genetically modified food due to the pollution of our earth?

I suppose what I am presenting in this book is kind of an "uphill battle."

1. The first step is for the reader to believe that the earth has changed from what God designed. People may say that such changes, i.e. transportation, technology, corporate farming, are for the better.
2. Possibly true, but as the second step the reader must believe that some changes are for the worst, i.e. toxic pollution, loss of animal habitat, polar ice melt.
3. The third step requires the reader to acknowledge that humans have acted on our environment- water, land, air, resources - in ways that have caused it to change.
4. Continuing on this uphill battle, the reader must admit that if some human actions are changed, the environment could improve, and become closer to God's design.
5. Next the reader must determine what personal changes could help.
6. Then, the reader must actually make these changes.
7. And finally, near the top of the hill, the reader looks for ways to help environmental organizations and/or to influence the government for higher level changes.

Where are you at in terms of these steps?

This study will lead the reader through God's amazing design for us and this planet as described in the bible. In contrast to each aspect of creation, I will offer images of earth today. The corresponding difficulties for humans will be presented. Finally, the reader will be asked to consider further action.

Action Steps: Influencing the market and worldwide industries by:
Supply and Demand - We should not feel like we are powerless. Each little action multiplied by MANY consumers changes the DEMAND. Before long, the suppliers will have to either increase or decrease their production. For example, if more consumers choose renewable power, the production will increase and prices will moderate, plus fossil fuel sources will lose market share.
Less consumption - The USA has the highest average per person consumption. This represents an excessive
impact on the environment. Buying only necessities and second hand items reduces environmental impact.
Writing to lawmakers - Letters to our representatives can influence policies. Imagine if the representative hears more from the opposite side, then supports measures against your views. Try to support your opinions with facts. Speak up about local issues, too.

(**NOTE**: The words "man" and "human" are always used in this book to denote BOTH man and woman.)

Lesson 1 - God's Vision of the Earth: First Day

My fear of the dark was very real. It enveloped six-year-old me when I needed to go into our basement at night. Even turning on the stairway light was not sufficient to take away all that lurked in the dark corners. I dreaded when one of my parents asked me to get something from the basement. Fortunately I am no longer afraid of the dark. Did you ever have a fear of the dark?

Despite humans' fear of the dark, God had a purpose for it. He started His creation of our planet with light and darkness.

1.   Read Genesis 1: 1-5. Describe God's accomplishments on the first day.

Not only did God separate light and darkness, He created a marker for each day. Why would He do this at this time?

2.   Consider Adam and Eve joining God's creation. What would they have been doing in the light? What would they have been doing in the darkness? What did God intend for man in this separation of light and darkness?

3.   Think about light and darkness in your life. In your daily life, what is the value of light? What is the value of darkness?

Light Pollution - When God looks down on the earth today He no longer sees simple darkness. He sees the many dots of light that humans have created, using some of the amazing components that He included on the earth. How did we get to this point, and is it good for us?

1.   In several places in the bible, there is mention of lamps for light. Read Exodus 25:37 (ESV): You shall make seven lamps for it. And the lamps shall be set up so as to give light on the space in front of it.

Yes, we did that! Not only to illuminate the altar, but to illuminate our buildings, our roads, our life! Do you think God intended for us to "light up our darkness" with many light bulbs?

2.   Just as in the Genesis creation accounting describing the seventh day as a day of rest, God designed humans for rest. Read each of these verses and note what God says about sleep:

        Psalm 127:2

        Psalm 4:8

        Proverbs 3:24

        Matthew 11:28-30

3.   Other than to consider going somewhere less bright to enable us to see the night sky, most of us would not acknowledge a light pollution problem. However, if our artificial lights are affecting the lives of animals and humans, then we are deviating from God's design. By lighting up what God designed as periods of darkness, we alter our biochemical rhythms.

God's brilliant design is evident in how humans and animals sleep. Sleep is not dependent on "emptying the mind," or even the physical act of lying down and stopping activity. Scientists have found that God designed us in such a way that DARKNESS sets off a chain reaction that results in melatonin production, a hormone that promotes sleep. At sundown photons strike the retina in the eye, sending signals through neurons to the brain's pineal gland, triggering production of melatonin. The melatonin hormone initiates many reactions: lowers body temperature, slows metabolism, activates circadian rhythms of sleep/wake cycles and increases leptin which reduces appetite.

Melatonin production is affected by light in two ways: light/darkness cycles modify its rhythm, and brief pulses of light abruptly stop its production. [1]   Too much light at bedtime will not allow those body changes, and too much light entering the room during the night will disrupt this process. When the body misses out on this natural process there are consequences:

        Based on a number of studies, low metabolism levels and circadian disruption are also
        thought to play a role in heart disease, diabetes, depression and cancer - particularly breast
        cancer...In 2007, the World Health Organization actually declared shift work a risk factor for
        cancer. And in 2012, the American Medical Association warned that pervasive use of
        nighttime lighting "creates potentially harmful health effects and/or hazardous situations." [2]

What do you think of God's amazing design for connecting darkness with the physiological changes for rest?

How well do you reduce light in the evening before you attempt to go to sleep?   Do you have any "light interruptions" through the night?

4.	Recently my husband and I considered buying new wall-mounted LED lights for our bedside. With these, we reasoned, either one of us could read later without disturbing the other. Then I learned about the problem with this idea... Unfortunately, LED TVs, computer screens and cell phones are very poor for reducing light, since they emit the blue, higher color temperature LED light. Perhaps you have heard it recommended that people stop "screen time" for some time before falling asleep. Preferably people should read with a dimmed energy-efficient incandescent bulb or a "warm white LED" from which the lower color temperature light is closer to darkness. Do you stop "screen time" well before trying to fall asleep? What type of light do you use at the bedside for reading?

5.	Animals are also affected by the excessive light. Again, God designed them so that the melatonin production increases leptin, a hormone that affects appetite. Since this same process happens for most animals at sundown, it is important that their appetite does not send them out foraging in the dark, when their camouflage is of little value. For nocturnal animals, with more artificial light in their environments, studies reveal fewer active hours.

In addition, many animals' life cycles depend on periods of darkness. The reproductive cycle of many animal species depends on the seasonal changes in light levels. Lemurs are such an animal. God's design for their reproduction depends again on melatonin. In the hours of long darkness of the winter, sexual activity is repressed. Conversely even in the winter, sexual activity increased for lemurs placed in conditions of extended artificial lighting. If lemurs get pregnant in the winter because of artificial lighting, then the pregnant mom and her eventual offspring could have difficulty acquiring food in the colder months. [3]

Another similar example is the tammar wallaby in Australia. This marsupial is most fertile as light starts fading at summer solstice. Their young are born six weeks later, when the fall harvest is abundant for their food requirements. A five year study of two wallaby populations showed that those living in the rural bush country followed these patterns, whereas the groups living by high-powered sodium lights always bore their young four weeks later. This affected the availability of food, leaving them to scavenge on area lawns. [4]
How could we help our animal populations survive on our lighted planet?

6.	Here is the case of the sea turtles that have been affected by light pollution. God created sea turtle hatchlings with the instinct to crawl toward the sea when they are hatched. In Florida, host to 90% of the US sea turtle population,man-made lights along the coastline attract the babies in the same manner that the moonlight reflected on the ocean waves should attract them. This leaves them vulnerable to predators and starvation as they wander on land, far from their proper destination. Some progress has been made in Florida to remedy this problem. Ideally all coastal lighting would be warmer, amber colored which does not attract the turtles, plus would be lower to the ground and more targeted.[5] Have you ever lived along a coastline? If you did, would you consider changing your lighting even if it meant higher cost?

7.   I have often heard the argument against ocean wind farms that their blades kill seabirds. I say, "Rotating windmill blades would be far less destructive than buildings."   Artificial light dramatically affects migratory birds. The attraction and glare of lights on buildings can be fatal to birds. In Canada citizens formed the Fatal Light Awareness Program to track bird deaths from building collisions. The founder estimates that Toronto buildings kill tens of thousands birds annually. Multiply this by other cities worldwide for a frightening picture.   How do you think God feels about birds dying in this manner? Do you believe government regulations should prohibit building lights at night and window coatings to reduce daytime collisions?

Conclude and Respond
In seeking to understand God's original design for our earth, this lesson focused on the first day of creation when God created light and darkness. Man subsequently created much artificial light to counteract the darkness, so much so that we could now consider it light pollution. The light pollution can interfere in God's design for man's and animal's natural cycles. This problem is one of many to be studied in this book.   Monitor this week how often you are viewing screens rather than incandescent or low color temperature light at bedtime. Also, determine if your sleep is disturbed by light. Pray that God will help you to identify and remedy any possible problem.

Lesson 1 – Action Steps
- For better sleep have less screen time at bedtime.
- Change to "warm white LED" for bedtime reading.
- Use warm, amber lights for outdoor lighting; cool blue lights confuse animals.
- Write to local, state and federal lawmakers to limit nighttime lighting in buildings.

[1] R Brennan, J E Jan & C J Lyon, "Light, Dark, and Melatonin: Emerging Evidence for the Importance of Melatonin in Ocular Physiology," Nature, September 22, 2006, https://www.nature.com/articles/6702597#:~:text=Melatonin%20is%20a%20hormone%2C%20which,cycles%2C%20thus%20regulating%20melatonin's%20secretion

[2] Nadia Drake, "Our Nights are Getting Brighter, and Earth Is Paying the Price," National Geographic, April 3, 2019, https://www.nationalgeographic.com/science/2019/04/nights-are-getting-brighter-earth-paying-the-price-light-pollution-dark-skies/

[3] Society for Experimental Biology. "Lights Out: Light Pollution Alters Reproduction Cycle in Lemurs," Science Daily, July 2, 2014, www.sciencedaily.com/releases/2014/07/140702203804.htm

[4] Drake, "Our Nights are Brighter."

[5] Drake, "Our Nights are Brighter."

Lesson 2 - God's Vision of the Earth: Second Day

Each time I watch the sky change at sunset I see the magnificence of God's design in our atmosphere. The atmosphere allows the light from the sun to pass through, giving us beautiful sunsets. In the previous lesson, we looked at Genesis 1:3: "Then God said, "Let there be light;' and there was light." Hidden in this simple statement is God's intricate imagining of the "colors" of light. God's design allows man to see light wavelengths from blue violet to red, the colors of the rainbow. These "wavelengths" are exactly what you might think: the distance from one peak to the next, which varies by color. Violet is the shortest, and red is the longest. To fully understand the sunset colors, we need to look closer at God's design for the atmosphere.

God's dome around the earth contains gas molecules, water droplets and dust particles. Light from the sun passes through this dome. In midday the sun is directly overhead, so the light path to us is the shortest. Because of this, the shorter wavelengths of visible light, the violet/blue, scatter the most, thus the sky looks blue.   At sunset the path of the sun's light passes through more of the atmosphere by the time it meets our eyes, causing the violet and blue to scatter more, so that these are out of our visible light. That leaves the longer wavelengths more visible to us. So, we see colors like yellow, orange, red. [1] The same phenomena happens at sunrise, in case you never witnessed it. We can thank God for His design!

1.   Describe your favorite sunset or sunrise.

2.   God's work on the second day involved separating the waters from the sky, or the heavens. Read this passage in Genesis 1:6-8. If possible contrast this passage as described in different editions of the Bible.   Note here the "parts" which God has separated:

3.   The Psalms in the bible are like poems in that they express ideas in few words. Read these two verses from Psalms, then comment on God's creation of "the heavens:"

Psalm 19:1

Psalm 89:11

Atmosphere

4.   - The New Revised Standard Version uses the word, "dome" to describe what is referred to as "sky" or "the heavens" in other versions. The idea of "dome" could be thought of as our atmosphere. God had an excellent design for the atmosphere. Here is a simple description of its role:

The atmosphere acts as a protective blanket for the Earth. Since, it is a bad conductor of heat, it keeps the average temperature of Earth fairly constant during the day and during the whole year. During the night, it causes the heat to escape into outer space. Therefore, the Earth receives correct amounts of heat at different times in a day due to the presence of atmosphere, which helps in climate control and allows living organisms to exist. [2]

Imagine the earth without this atmosphere. Describe what you think it would be like.

5.   Because God's design focused on a place for humans to live, His atmosphere's design enables us to do that. It acts as a blanket around the earth, keeping the temperature "liveable" for humans. To do this, the air contains a balanced mix of gases nitrogen, oxygen, argon and carbon dioxide. This mix of gases also protects us from the harmful ultraviolet rays from the sun, solar wind and cosmic rays.   Since creation, the precise balance in the atmosphere has been maintained until the last century.

Look at God's command to man in Genesis 1:28. What did God tell man to do with His creation?

What has man done to "subdue" and "have dominion" over the earth?

Atmosphere Composition

6.   - Perhaps you have heard the terms for years: "greenhouse gases" and "global warming." Unless you have studied these terms, you probably have a vague understanding. Also, you may have skepticism about these concepts. You are reading this bible study book, so your goal may be to have a better understanding.

God designed the earth's atmosphere with a balance of gases in order to achieve an environment in which humans could thrive. Earth's atmosphere is composed of about 78% nitrogen, 21% oxygen, and 0.93% argon. The remainder, less than 0.1%, contains such trace gases as carbon dioxide, nitrous oxide, methane and ozone. (The percentages do vary slightly, thus, the use of "about.") [3]

You have probably heard of concerns about increasing carbon dioxide levels. What has happened over the past two centuries is that the presence of "trace" gases has increased dramatically. In addition, man-made fluorinated gases have been added. We can look at these numbers to show us how our current gas composition is different.   Although I recommend that you look at the graphs on this webpage (Reference link for graphs: "Climate Change Indicators: Atmospheric Concentrations of Greenhouse Gases," US Environmental Protection Agency, https://www.epa.gov/climate-indicators/climate-change-indicators-atmospheric-concentrations-greenhouse-gases), I have extracted some data to complete this table [4] :

Gas	800,000 to 1 BCE	1 AD	1950AD	2015 AD
Carbon Dioxide	230 ppm (average)	260 ppm	310 ppm	400 ppm
Methane	500 ppb (average)	600 ppb	1250 ppb	1800 ppb
Nitrous Oxide	250 ppb (average)	260 ppb	285 ppb	325 ppb

7.   Notice that for a very long time, from 800,000 BC to Christ's birth, the level of these trace gases had changed very little. Then, from Christ's birth to 1950 the levels have increased, with methane more than doubling. By 2015 the carbon dioxide has almost doubled, the methane has tripled and the nitrous oxide has increased by about one-third.   Why do you think this balance in the atmosphere has not been maintained in the last century? What has changed in those years that could have affected the balance?

8.   What have you heard about the reason for the increased accumulation of these gases in the atmosphere? What do you think has caused it?

God certainly designed the balanced atmosphere for man's well-being. What do you think God thinks about this change in His design for our atmosphere?

Ozone

9.   Ozone is like tomato sauce: It is good for it to be on your plate, but not good for it to be on your shirt. The good place for ozone is in the upper atmosphere. As it surrounds the earth it prohibits

harmful UV rays from the sun to make it to the earth. For a few decades ozone-depletion was in the news as gases like chlorofluorocarbons destroyed the ozone over the South Pole. Because of the potential bad effects from UV rays reaching the earth, these destroyers have been banned. Their replacement, hydrochlorofluorocarbons, while harmful, is far less potent. Production of these also has been nearly eliminated internationally through governmental action, except that developing countries are permitted to continue use until 2030. The negative effects of the ozone hole include skin cancer, eye cataracts and immune deficiency disorders. [5]

The bad place for ozone is at ground level. In fact, "ground-level ozone warnings" are commonly issued in smog areas.   Although it is not generated as ozone, it is formed from emissions of nitrogen oxide, volatile organic compounds plus sunlight. Nitrogen oxide comes from combustion of coal and oil in power plants and from vehicles. VOCs are emitted from paints, aerosol sprays, cleaners and pesticides. Ground-level ozone primarily affects lung tissue and lung function, worsening conditions like bronchitis, emphysema, and asthma.[6]

Have you ever had a ground-level ozone warning (or air quality alert) in your area? In light of auto and power plant emissions, plus the listed VOC-emitters being the culprits for this pollutant, what could you do to help?

Temperatures

10.   These additional gases trap heat in the atmosphere around the earth. Trapped heat around the earth causes our global temperature average to be warmer.   You may say, "We have had many below zero days in our area. Plus, temperatures this spring have been below average." It is difficult to picture what is happening worldwide with our limited experience.   My son lives in Europe, so he experienced the severe summer temperatures in 2019. He said that most evenings the temperatures did not fall below 80. So, the nighttime low temperatures also impact the average.

Here are a few numbers:
- Antarctica reached 64.9°F on 2/6/2020. Previous record was: 63.5 °F on 3/24/2015 [7]
- Paris recorded the high of 108.7°F on 8/29/2019. During the same heat wave, The Netherlands reached 105.2 °F, and Germany hit 108.7 °F. [8]
- Greatest Temperature anomalies worldwide:
    Globally, 2019 temperatures were second only to those of 2016 and continued the planet's long-term warming trend: the past five years have been the warmest of the last 140 years. This past year, they were 1.8 degrees Fahrenheit (0.98 degrees Celsius) warmer than the 1951 to 1980 mean, according to scientists at NASA's Goddard Institute for Space Studies (GISS) in New York. [9]

11.   Do you agree or disagree with the conclusion that the global average temperature is increasing?   If you agree, what do you think has caused the global average temperature to increase?

12.   I will simply describe our current environmental condition: Gases which God placed in the atmosphere in trace amounts have accumulated in larger quantities in the last 150 years. These gases act differently than God's original design for the atmosphere: They trap some of the sun's heat in the air around the earth. The same idea applies in construction: If you have an "energy audit" of your home you may be told to add more insulation and/or add weather stripping by openings. The goal is to keep the atmosphere of your home, whether it be warm or cool, contained. These extra gases in our atmosphere act as insulation or weather stripping, keeping the sun's heat energy contained. More heat energy contained means warmer temperatures.

Perhaps you still do not believe that the earth is warmer, regardless of temperature data I have presented. There are other facts I can give you. If global temperatures have not changed, then ice caps on mountains and glaciers in the polar regions should not have changed. The World Glacier Monitoring Service studied 42 reference glaciers to find that, "Cumulative ice loss between 1980 and 2018 is −21.7 meters of water equivalent, the equivalent of cutting a 24-m (79-foot) thick slice off the top of the each glacier." [10]

If global temperatures have not changed, then hurricanes should be acting the same as they did hundreds of years ago. Unfortunately, there is limited data about hurricanes over 100 years ago. However, it is true that storms over warmer ocean water move more slowly, and consequently pick up more moisture. One analysis concluded that by the latter 21st century Atlantic hurricanes will be 4% more intense and produce 10 to 15 % more rainfall in the area of the hurricane. [11]

Do these sound like insignificant changes?

Man and Fossil Fuels

13.   Perhaps you do not believe that man has played a role in this change. You cannot deny that humans use more inventions that require power now than they did in 1900 (Unless you survive on a deserted island, in which case I do not know how you could be reading this.). You pull into the local gas station, fill up, then drive hundreds of miles on that gasoline. You plug in your television to the electric outlet, which is fed from the local power station, so that you can watch your favorite shows. You fire up your gas grill with the propane tank you purchased at the hardware store, and soon you are enjoying grilled chicken. You accept a package which the delivery man pulls from his gasoline-powered truck, that you ordered on your plugged-in computer.

The gasoline, propane and possibly the electricity come from fuel that has been extracted from the earth. How did that fuel form within the earth? What was God's design in forming fuel underground? Coal, oil and gas are organic material which has been compressed within the earth for thousands of years. The heat and pressure within the earth cause the hydrogen and oxygen to be squished out as gas or water, leaving primarily carbon.[12]

So, think of Adam and Eve in the Garden of Eden. How did that lush garden end up underground to be compressed into carbon-based fuels? Scientists know that organic material deposits in the earth had to be vast enough to create the fuels existing in the earth today. They believe that such vast quantities were buried through flood deposits and volcanic ash layers. Do you have any guesses about how this may have happened?

14. "Flood…" Does that idea "ring a bell?" Readers of the Old Testament would think of the world-wide flood described in Genesis 7:11-12, 17-24. Not only did the flood waters consume plant life, but people, animals, creatures and birds were wiped from the earth.   Genesis 8:3 notes that the waters receded steadily. As the waters flowed quickly back into oceans and seas, sediments of dead plant and animal life were left in layers on the land. Add to this many, many years of compression and heat to give us our underground supply of fossil fuels.

As you would guess, some skeptics do not believe that the great flood could have yielded the quantity of fossil fuels present in the earth. Dr. Andrew Snelling documented his analysis of this.[13] There have certainly been other floods and volcanic eruptions over time which may have helped create the necessary deposits. Do you believe that the great flood in Genesis would have been sufficient to produce all of the earth's fossil fuels?   Do you believe that God planned these deposits for such a time as now when man would be so dependent on energy?

Global Warming

15. Going a step further, when these carbon-based fuels are extracted from the earth, then burned for our energy needs, the carbon is released into the air. It may seem that what is in the air could not really impact us. But by adding this carbon to a precisely balanced atmosphere, the atmosphere behaves differently. It releases less of the sun's reflected heat into space. More of the sun's heat stays around the earth. Thus, we go from the flood's deposit of sediments, to a warmer planet, or global warming. Do you believe that God anticipated humans' use of fossil fuel and the resulting warming of our atmosphere?

Do you feel that God would want us to slow down this trend?   Or, do you feel that God sees this as a progression to some end of the earth?

Conclude and Respond

Think about the necessities of life: food, water, shelter, rest…any others? The planet we live on was designed by God in such a manner that it could sustain human life long-term. By placing earth a precise distance from the sun, God knew that our environment would have the proper solar radiation for man's survival. However, He needed to create the atmosphere around the planet so that the solar heat and radiation would be perfect for us.   So, we should add to the list of necessities, "atmosphere."

This lesson brought to light changes in God's exact balance of atmospheric gases. Humans have added more gases, called the "greenhouse gases." This change has led to improper amounts of solar radiation being held in our atmosphere, or "global warming." The result is warmer temperatures.

Consider this week what you believe is man's role in "global warming." Pray and ask God for clearer understanding of temperature change, including man's role. .

Lesson 2 – Action Steps
- To reduce Nitrogen Oxide, drive less; use mass transit and/or drive electric or hybrid car.
- Change composition of atmosphere to match God's design by using fewer fossil fuels. Ideas for how to do this: eat less beef; use "manual" tools rather than power tools; plant more trees; choose renewable power source from your electricity provider, or install solar panels; etc.

[1] University of Wisconsin - Madison, "What Determines Sky's Colors At Sunrise And Sunset?," ScienceDaily, November 15, 2007, https://www.sciencedaily.com/releases/2007/11/071108135522.htm#:~:text=Summary%3A,rays%2C%20causing%20them%20to%20scatter.

[2] LokeshCBSE,"State the Role of Atmosphere in Climate Control," Discourse, CBSE Class 9, April 2019, https://ask.learncbse.in/t/state-the-role-of-atmosphere-in-climate-control/44018.

[3] Encyclopedia.com, s.v. "Atmosphere, Composition and Structure," accessed August 22, 2020, https://www.encyclopedia.com/science/encyclopedias-almanacs-transcripts-and-maps/atmosphere-composition-and-structure.

[4] "Climate Change Indicators: Atmospheric Concentrations of Greenhouse Gases," prepared by US Environmental Protection Agency, (April 2016), https://www.epa.gov/climate-indicators/climate-change-indicators-atmospheric-concentrations-greenhouse-gases.

[5] Wikipedia, s.v. "Chlorofluorocarbon, " accessed September 2020, https://en.wikipedia.org/wiki/Chlorofluorocarbon#:~:text=Since%20the%20late%201970s%2C%20the,effects%20on%20the%20ozone%20layer.&text=In%201978%2C%20under%20the%20Toxic,of%20CFCS%20and%20aerosol%20propellants.)

[6] Adrien Lafond, "What are the Main Sources of Nitrogen Oxides and Volatile Organic Compounds?" prepared by Airboxlab US, accessed September 2020, https://foobot.io/guides/what-are-the-main-sources-of-nitrogen-oxides-and-volatile-organic-compounds.php

[7] Derrick Bryson Taylor, "Antarctica Sets Record High Temperature: 64.9 Degrees," New York Times, February 8, 2020, https://www.nytimes.com/2020/02/08/climate/antarctica-record-temperature.html.

[8] Eric Leister and Kristina Pydynowski, "Paris Breaks All-Time High Temperature As Deadly Heat Wave Shatters Records Across Europe," AccuWeather, July 25, 2019, https://www.accuweather.com/en/weather-news/paris-on-alert-for-record-breaking-temperatures-as-heat-wave-grips-spain-to-germany/461396.

[9] Lori Perkins, "Global Temperature Anomalies from 1880 to 2019," prepared by Scientific Visualization Studio, NASA, January 15, 2020, https://svs.gsfc.nasa.gov/4787.

[10] Rebecca Lindsey, "Climate Change: Glacier Mass Balance, " prepared by Climate.gov, National Oceanic and Atmospheric Administration (February 14, 2020), https://www.climate.gov/news-features/understanding-climate/climate-change-glacier-mass-balance.

[11] "Global Warming and Hurricanes," prepared by Geophysical Fluid Dynamics Laboratory, Sept. 18, 2020, https://www.gfdl.noaa.gov/global-warming-and-hurricanes/#global-warming-and-atlantic-hurricanes.

[12] Lance Ponder, "Fossil Fuel," Bible.org, August 29, 2011, https://bible.org/seriespage/18-fossil-fuel

[13] Andrew Snelling, Dr., "Coal Beds and Noah's Flood," Answers in Genesis.org, June 1, 1986, https://answersingenesis.org/geology/catastrophism/coal-beds-and-noahs-flood/).

Lesson 3 - God's Vision of the Earth on the Third Day: Water

Niagara Falls is perhaps the most amazing natural site I have ever seen. So, for my second opportunity to see it, I was not going to let a snowstorm the night before stop our 7-hour drive there. The near zero degree temperatures provided an extra spectacle: the partially frozen layers of falling water. What draws my attention is the tremendous force of force of water cascading over the cliffs. That powerful force of water continually carves the underlying rock, gradually changing the look of the falls. I am curious what the cliffs looked like long ago, and what the shape of the falls took back then. What did falls such as these look like when God first separated the waters and the dry land?

1. Pondering this leads me to the question: What purpose did God have for waterfalls? What purpose did He have for such powerful rivers?

2. Another very beautiful image I have in my mind is Silent Valley Reservoir in Ireland. My image from our March trip there is stately barren mountains guarding the serene crystal blue expanse of water. The lack of tourists that day contributed to the incredible feeling of stillness.

Read Psalm 23:2-3. What does the psalmist derive from still waters?

3. At this stage in creation the earth is apparently only water and atmosphere, so God continues his work to add land and vegetation. His work is described in these verses: Genesis 1:9-13. Read these.

4. God gathered the waters together. Man has classified the largest bodies of salt water as the four oceans, Atlantic, Pacific, Indian and Arctic. In God's design some oceans are larger than others, warmer than others, but all contain salt water which is not potable. Also by his design, the inland bodies of water are not salt water and provide us our drinking water. Why would God design these two types of water?

Think about creatures which live in the oceans like sea bass, versus those which can only survive in freshwater like catfish and trout. Do you like salmon? These fish live part of their lives in freshwater, and part in salty ocean water. God had an amazing plan, even for fish. Why would God design fish in such a manner?

5.   When I was a child our property backed up to a park. The most exciting part of this park, notwithstanding the playground, was the stream that coursed through it. "We are going to the creek," my siblings and I would announce to mom. She had no fear of our adventures here because this "stream" was at most two feet wide and 10 inches deep. Whether our fascination was the frogs, the ever-flowing cool water, or the crawdads hiding under rocks, we certainly enjoyed God's creation!

Read these verses relating to God's creation of freshwater:

    Genesis 2:5-6

    Genesis 2:10-14

From these verses, what do you think was God's purpose for rivers and streams?

6.   Isaiah 49:10 further describes God's purpose for "springs of water." Read it, then note the additional purpose.

7.   One might also ask: why did God create two types of water on the earth: salty ocean water and freshwater? Here are a few verses relating God's purpose for salt water in seas and oceans. Read each, then note the described purpose.

    Psalm 148:7

    Ezekiel 26:4 - 5

In creating the various bodies of water, God had an ingenious design. Salt water can support unique sea life, whereas fresh water can support different fish and amphibians. God designed a precise balance in each body of water. Unfortunately, this balance gets upset when arctic ice melt, which is fresh water, floods the salty ocean. Changes in salinity in one area of the ocean cause ocean life there to relocate, or, if not possible, to die.

Ocean Currents

8.   Not only did God create the two types of water for different species, He designed a complex system of ocean currents that direct our weather worldwide. The ocean currents are caused by five large systems of circular currents and strong winds, called gyres. In the case of the Gulf Stream, if all is going as designed, the warm water in the Gulf of Mexico flows northward, warming the east coast of the United States and the western area of Europe. This warm water flow pushes down the colder, denser water in a south-bound flow. "If all is going as designed" is an important caveat. With global warming and the melt of glacial, land ice on Greenland, fresh water flows into the path of the Gulf Stream, diluting its salinity and decreasing its density changing the flow of the Gulf Stream. This alters the climate of these regions. The entire balance God designed for the Gulf Stream is upset.

The Antarctic Circumpolar Current connects the Atlantic Ocean, the Pacific Ocean and the Indian Oceans, thus its God-designed balance is important to all of these bodies of water. Warming of the atmosphere and of the oceans has impacted this current. Also, the warmer bodies of water adjoining the ocean feed it and affect the current. At the same time, the melting land ice from Antarctica sends fresh water in, making the water less dense. Both the upper layers and the deepest layers of the Southern Ocean are warmer and fresher on average in this decade. Again, the entire balance God designed for the Antarctic Circumpolar Current is upset.[1]

Have you ever vacationed in the Southern Hemisphere where the oceans are warmed by the Antarctic Circumpolar Current? How do you think God feels about this balance being upset?

9.   God set up currents in the ocean in order to allow heated up waters from the warmer areas of the earth to flow to the cooler areas. He accomplished this through winds, tides, water temperature and water density. Surface currents, which we feel and see in waves and rip currents, are formed by winds. (Remember that winds are formed from the movement of air masses of different temperatures.)

If you traveled on a boat further out into the ocean you would still feel surface currents. God designed the earth to spin on its axis, which caused wind patterns around the globe described by scientists as the Coriolis Effect. It is really ingenious on God's part to have the winds in the northern hemisphere curve to the right, while those in the southern hemisphere curve to the left. This design causes the ocean to flow in clockwise pattern in the north and a counterclockwise pattern in the south.[2]

It seems that God's plan for the current in the Atlantic Ocean was to moderate coastal temperatures in Florida, while warming western Europe. Have you ever vacationed in Florida? If so, what were the daily temperatures? Have you vacationed in western Europe? What were the average temperatures there during your stay?

Here is a chart I created to help you see the effect of the Gulf Stream.   In case you do not remember what "latitude" is, it is a horizontal measure for a location on the globe, with 0° latitude at the Equator, and 90° at the poles.   Notice the relatively warmer temperatures in western European cities at the same latitudes as American cities. [3]

North American city (latitude)	Average High/Low annual temps (°F)	City in western Europe (latitude)	Average High/Low annual temps (°F)
New York City (40.7 °)	84° / 39°	Madrid (40.4°)	89° / 50°
St. Johns, Newfoundland (47.5 °)	68°/ 31°	Paris (48.85°)	78 °/ 46 °
Cape Cod (41.67°)	79°/ 38°	Rome (41.9°)	89 °/ 54°
Halifax , Nova Scotia, Canada (44.6 °)	73°/32°	Venice, Italy (45.4°)	83 °/ 45°

Reflect this ocean current situation to the southern hemisphere, and we see the benefit/damage to Antarctica: the benefit of warmer waters can support diverse plant and animal life, but the warmer waters melt the bottom layers of ice shelves, threatening the stability of them.

God has created ocean currents for a perfect balance of the oceans and the adjoining lands. So, imagine what could happen if the air temperatures or the ocean water temperatures get warmer. Do you think this could impact God's perfect balance? What might happen to the warmer areas of western Europe?

What might happen to Antarctica, both the ocean life and the ice shelves?

Marine Heat Waves

10.   Here is another aspect of God's intended design for earth: Water on the earth absorbs heat from the air. This has always been good for the air. That is, the global warming of our atmosphere is reduced by the oceans' absorption of heat. In fact, ninety percent of additional heat from man's use of fossil fuels is trapped in the oceans. [4]

Warmer air causes warmer oceans, leading to "marine heat waves" around the world. The Mediterranean Sea has had heat waves in 2012, 2015, 2017 and 2018. In 2018 the ocean waters around New Zealand contained an area of 130000 square miles of hot water. As of April 2020, warm waters at the Uruguayan coast killed much of their resource of mussels and clams.   Also, for centuries the waters around the Australian island of Tasmania hosted 9 million square miles of kelp. By early 2020 this had shrunk to 500,000 square miles due to warmer waters. [5]   One more example: on the western side of Antarctica the ocean temperature has risen 5° F from 1950 to 2017. [6]

What problems are posed by a warmer ocean?   Warmer waters expand, contributing to sea level rise. Warmer water is less able to absorb carbon dioxide from the atmosphere. Warmer water impacts ocean currents, and, thus, weather. Warmer water is more acidic, which not only impacts the survival of species like algae but decays the shells of ocean life.   For example, the thin shells of pteropods, which are the food source for sea life from seabirds to whales, are subject to decay. Loss of this species would impact much ocean fishing. So, warmer waters affect food chains and biodiversity. Cod fishing in Alaskan waters and shrimp fishing near Maine have both been greatly affected by reduced volume and relocation. [7]   Do you eat any ocean fish, such as halibut, cod, red snapper, mahi mahi, grouper? How would you feel if that fish was no longer available?

"The Blob"

11.   The ocean water absorbs excess heat from the atmosphere. However, the northern Pacific Ocean saw unusual warming starting in 2013 over a 1000 mile stretch which showed temperatures 5.4 to 10.8 degrees Fahrenheit above normal. This warming continued through 2016, intensifying with El Nino in 2015. Its name, "The Blob," disguises its destruction. Production of microscopic algae severely decreased, robbing many sea creatures from shrimp to whales of their food supply, while simultaneously the warming increased the metabolism of salmon, cod and halibut, causing them to eat more than usual. Nearly one million seabirds which depend on fish for food died from summer of 2015 to spring of 2016. Imagine the scene: 62000 murres (sea birds) dead on the seashores from Alaska to Washington. In addition, harmful algae blooms killed many animals and impacted the fishing industry.[8]

Unfortunately, this was not a fluke, but the start of a pattern. Another blob of similar size formed in September 2019 off of the coast of Washington. Picture another such blob in 2020 which is larger than Texas currently off of the eastern coast of New Zealand. In each case the impact on sea life will be immense. These are not isolated incidents because:

> From 1982 to 2016, there was an 82% rise in the number of heat wave days on the global ocean surface, according to a 2018 study. [9]

Do you see any danger if such blobs continue to form? What would God think about these blobs?

Does man have any responsibility for changing the balance of the oceans?

Ice

12.   God created the ice on the earth, too. Read Job 37:10 ESV):
         By the breath of God ice is given, and the broad waters are frozen fast.

Why do you think God's plan for Earth included ice?

Did you realize that when the ice cube in your glass melts, the level of the fluid is not changed? Ice floating in water displaces (pushes aside) water so that when it melts it does not raise the level. Ice in the Arctic Ocean is like this: it floats on the ocean, so if it melts it will not change sea level.   In contrast, land ice works differently: Let your "glacier" land ice cube melt in a separate glass, then pour it into the first glass, the water level rises. This is how the melting of land ice works, such as from Greenland and Antarctica: it raises the water level of the ocean. There is evidence that land ice has been melting in Greenland, Antarctica and other land glaciers. In Glacier National Park (Montana) by 2017 only 26 of the 150 glaciers remained. [10]   Cumulative ice loss between 1980 and 2018 is −21.7 meters of water equivalent, the equivalent of cutting a 24-m (79-foot) thick slice off the top of each glacier. [11]

There are a few causes for the melting ice. Obviously, if the temperature of the air is high enough in the areas of land ice, then the ice will melt.   Also, if warmer ocean water meets the ice, then it will melt there. Additionally, sunshine will melt the surfaces. Greenland experienced unusually extensive melting in 2019 because of an unusually high pressure weather pattern. HIgh pressure weather means fewer clouds, and thus, more sunshine on the ice surfaces. [12]

Not so obvious is the problem of the melting ice shelf.   The ice shelf floats on the sea, but is securely attached to the land ice. These are common all around Antarctica and Greenland. Warmer ocean water acts on the lower layer of the shelf, gradually weakening its integrity. If it breaks off, then the glacier behind it is no longer supported.   Did you ever put some items in a cabinet, then quickly close the door? The next time you go to open it you might be surprised to have the items fall out! The ice shelf and the glacier work the same way. The ice shelf is the closed cabinet door, holding the "items" - the glacier ice - in place. Bottom line: we do not want the ice shelves to melt and break off. In 2016 a huge part of the Pine Island Glacier in Antarctica broke off in this manner. [13]

Also contributing to the weakening of glaciers is surface ice melt. As pools are formed from the ice melt, the tendency is for the water to flow toward crevasses in the glacier. Like with any crack, more pressure only increases the stress on the crevasse, leading to ultimate breakage. So, more melted water flowing into crevasses will ultimately cause breakage of the ice.

The verse noted above from Job 37:10 is one of the few mentions in the bible about God creating ice. Do you believe that God designed the ice on the earth? If so, it may have existed for millions of years in the form as God designed it. How does God feel about much ice melting in the last few decades?

Floods

13.   One afternoon last summer my husband and I went to an indoor show at the New Jersey shore. A storm passed over the theater during the show, however, what we found when we emerged frightened us. Approaching our car we could see that the six-inch deep flooding was a mere half inch below the underbody of my car. We hurriedly hopped in, then I slowly drove on flooded streets for blocks. Fortunately we were able to follow the locals to a street on higher ground and avoid any damage. The scariest part was that we heard from locals that this is a frequent occurrence in recent years with every storm.

Like this NJ coastal area, places like Miami, Fl, also experience such flooding:

> When the flooding is really bad, water doesn't just fill the streets outside Manolo Pedraza's house. It bubbles up through a shower drain. Pedraza lives in Shorecrest, a northern Miami neighborhood that faces flooding so regularly it happens even when it hasn't rained. All it takes to fill the streets to knee-high depth on those days is a full moon. The flood comes up through storm drains, making it impossible to navigate without encountering the water, which is mixed with sewage and whatever else it picked up along the way. [14]

Do you think there was coastal flooding during the time of Adam and Eve?   Why do you think there is coastal flooding in recent years?   What has happened to make the coastal situation different from God's design?

14.   Flooding represents TOO MUCH water in an area, while drought represents too little.   Read Isaiah 44:3:

> For I will pour water on the thirsty land, and streams on the dry ground; I will pour my Spirit upon your offspring, and my blessing on your descendants. (ESV)

What do you think this verse says about dry land?   Would God allow drought?

Perhaps you look at the second half of the verse and believe God is using the "streams on the dry ground" figuratively ONLY to refer to God sending His blessings and Spirit on descendants. If so, could the "water on the thirsty land," be a blessing for His people?

15. The psalmist writes about God's role in floods and drought in Psalm 74:15:
> You broke open the fountain and the **flood**; You dried up mighty rivers.

Also consider Job 12:15:
> If he holds back the waters, there is drought; if he lets them loose, they devastate the land.

For what reasons would God send a flood, or a drought?

Has your town ever been in a drought emergency? What aspects of your life did you need to change?

Drought

16. Cape Town, South Africa, was in a drought emergency in 2018. The city warned that a "Day Zero" would arrive, when low reservoir levels would require tap water to be turned off, with limited water available at regional sites. In anticipation of this catastrophe people were asked to make drastic changes, such as flushing the toilet only once-daily, and taking 90-second showers over a bucket for reuse. As you might imagine, this directive prompted hoarding, civil unrest and reduced tourist interest. But, it worked; the crisis was averted! People changed their habits, and maintained the limit of 50 liters per day per person. In 2019-2020, governments are devising comprehensive strategies for water use considering population growth, agricultural use, and water sustainability. [15]

Average daily water user per American is 330 liters. Could you imagine living with only 50 liters per day? What do you think Americans would do with similar restrictions?

God designed Cape Town's area as an oasis surrounded by desert. He placed Table Mountain in such a way to stall the Atlantic Ocean breezes, yielding regular abundant rainfall. This long-standing design became impacted with drier weather, less winter rainfall and reduced stream flows, all likely results of climate change as seen worldwide. City planners did not expect the resulting multi-year drought. The balance between supply and demand was upset. [16]

Read Job 12:15. Did God allow the years of drought? Does He allow droughts in other cities, Mexico City, Melbourne (Australia), Jakarta (Indonesia), São Paulo (Brazil), Los Angeles?

17. **Aral Sea, Russia** - By God's design, the Aral Sea in southwestern Russia was the fourth largest sea in the world in 1950 and its fish contributed to the food supply of Russia. It was in balance, being fed by rainwater and two rivers. In the 1960s the Russian government diverted the two rivers for agriculture purposes, using 45 dams, 80 reservoirs and 20,000 miles of canals. [17]   Although this turned the surrounding desert into productive cropland, it severely affected the Aral Sea.

> In the first decade, the salinity increased by 14%, which exceeded the threshold for many commercial fish. As a result commercial fishing catches fell from 43,430 tons in 1960 to zero in 1980. [18]

Inadequate attempts have been made to restock fish in the North Aral Sea, where a dam has helped. In addition to the loss of fish, other impacts are: the size of the sea is one-tenth of its original size; contaminated dust from dried out agriculture fields regularly blows across the region affecting public health; remaining water is increasingly saltier and polluted from fertilizer and pesticides; summers are hotter and drier and winters are colder due to loss of the influence of the large body of water.

What does God think when He looks at the Aral Sea? What could the Russians have done differently to reduce the effect?

Conclude and Respond

From Niagara Falls to the snow-capped mountains God conceived our planet to have ice sheets in frigid places, ocean currents in orchestrated patterns and lakes for relaxing fishing trips. Instead we have melting glaciers, disturbed currents and salty lakes. Certainly God saw this coming. But what does He see in the future? Does He see the end of glacial melt, the return to freshwater lakes, and ocean currents supporting marine life as intended? I hope so.

When you talk to God this week tell him how beautiful the waterfall, or the stream or the ocean was when you last saw it. Ask Him to help us solve these problems as quickly as possible. Ask Him to help us communicate with others about the way our world is changing.

Lesson 3 – Action Steps

- Regularly reduce water use to help reduce drought: use cup for teeth rinsing; take shorter/fewer showers;   avoid overwatering of lawn; buy water-saving appliances.
- Reduce sea-level rise by reducing global warming (Choose renewable energy supplier, eat less beef, drive less or use electric vehicle, use "manual" tools.).

[1] Beth Daley, "Explainer: how the Antarctic Circumpolar Current helps keep Antarctica frozen", by Beth Daley, The Conversation, November 15, 2018, https://theconversation.com/explainer-how-the-antarctic-circumpolar-current-helps-keep-antarctica-frozen-106164

[2] Jennifer Horton, " How Ocean Currents Work," How Stuff Works, accessed August 2020, https://science.howstuffworks.com/environmental/earth/oceanography/ocean-current2.htm

[3] "Browse 41,997 CITIES WORLDWIDE," accessed September 2020, https://www.weatherbase.com/

[4] Damian Carrington, "Ocean temperatures hit record high as rate of heating accelerates," The Guardian, January 13, 2020, https://www.theguardian.com/environment/2020/jan/13/ocean-temperatures-hit-record-high-as-rate-of-heating-accelerates)

[5] Jeff Goodell, "Rising Tides, Troubled Waters," Rolling Stone, April 2020, p. 66.

[6] Douglas Fox, "The Crisis in the Ice," National Geographic, July 2017, p. 38.

[7] Goodell, "Rising Tides, Troubled Waters," p. 66-67.

[8] Jessie Yeung, "A Blob of Hot Water in the Pacific Ocean Killed a Million Seabirds, Scientists Say," CNN World, January 16, 2020, https://www.cnn.com/2020/01/16/world/blob-seabird-study-intl-hnk-scli-scn/index.html)

[9] Yeung, "Blob of Hot Water," January 16, 2020.

[10] Oliver Milman, "US Glacier National Park Losing Its Glaciers With Just 26 of 150 Left," The Guardian, May 11, 2017, https://www.theguardian.com/environment/2017/may/11/us-glacier-national-park-is-losing-its-glaciers-with-just-26-of-150-left#:~:text=Some%20have%20lost%20as%20much,19th%20century%2C%20only%2026%20remain.

[11] Rebecca Lindsey, "Climate Change: Glacier Mass Balance," Prepared by Climate.gov, February 14, 2020, https://www.climate.gov/news-features/understanding-climate/climate-change-glacier-mass-balance

[12] Nicola Davis, "Scientists Confirm Dramatic Melting of Greenland Ice Sheet," The Guardian, April 15, 2020, https://www.theguardian.com/science/2020/apr/15/scientists-confirm-dramatic-melting-greenland-ice-sheet

[13] Fox, "The Crisis in the Ice," July 2017.

[14] Kevin Loria, "Miami Is Racing Against Time to Keep Up With Sea Level Rise," Business Insider, April 12, 2018, https://www.businessinsider.com/miami-floods-sea-level-rise-solutions-2018-4

[15] Krista Mahr, "How Cape Town Was Saved From Running Out Of Water," The Guardian, May 4, 2018, https://www.theguardian.com/world/2018/may/04/back-from-the-brink-how-cape-town-cracked-its-water-crisis

[16] Craig Welch, "Why Cape Town Is Running Out Of Water and Who Is Next?" National Geographic, March 5, 2018, https://www.nationalgeographic.com/news/2018/02/cape-town-running-out-of-water-drought-taps-shutoff-other-cities/

[17] Paul Andrews, "Who Drained Russia's Vast Aral Sea?" Wordpress.com, April 30, 2018, https://paulwandrews.wordpress.com/2018/04/30/who-drained-russias-vast-aral-sea/

[18] Thompson, "The Aral Sea Crisis," Columbia.edu, accessed July, 2020, http://www.columbia.edu/~tmt2120/environmental%20impacts.htm)

Lesson 4 - God's Vision of the Earth on the Third Day: Land

One evening when I was twenty-something I rode with two colleagues eastbound on I-80 from Sacramento to Lake Tahoe. My surprise at finding out - with $20 cash in my purse - that there were casinos there, was dwarfed by an even bigger surprise. The magnificence of the mountains along the route was like nothing I had ever experienced. As we wound through the narrow mountain passes, each turn brought a more breathtaking view. The lush evergreen forests and the snow caps spread over God's spectacular canvas, culminating in the most picturesque: the serene lake framed by stately mountains. Since then I have viewed many more mountains, cliffs and hills, and am always amazed at God's handiwork. This is all part of what He accomplished on the third day.

1. On the third day God separated the land from the water as we read in Genesis 1:9-10:
> And God said, "Let the waters under the heavens be gathered together into one place, and let the dry land appear." And it was so. God called the dry land Earth, and the waters that were gathered together he called Seas. And God saw that it was good.

Psalm 104:5-14 depicts God's arrangement of the waters and the mountains. Read this passage.

Think of a place you have seen that resembles what the psalmist describes. What value do mountains and valleys have in your life? Do you ever spend time in such places for refreshment?

2. As God pulled the waters together, he let the dry land appear, which He called Earth. Man has classified the largest bodies of land as continents: North America, South America, Africa, Asia, Europe, Australia and Antarctica. Each of these continents has been designed to host specific kinds of plant and animal life. Job 8:11 says:
> Can papyrus grow where there is no marsh? Can reeds flourish where there is no water?

Also, people cannot easily live in some areas, such as Antarctica. Why would God have arranged the land masses in this manner?

What do you think was God's design for people being able to inhabit the entire earth, in light of starting with one couple in the Garden of Eden? How would God envision people migrating from one continent to another?

3.   God designed the land to be fertile, as Genesis 27:28 describes:
May God give you dew from heaven and make your fields fertile! May he give you plenty of grain and wine!

Deuteronomy 8:10 tells of what God has given to His people and what He desires from them:
You will have all you want to eat, and you will give thanks to the Lord your God for the fertile land that he has given you.

In giving us fertile land, what is God giving to us? What are we to do in response?

Agriculture

4.   Land has been used for agriculture ever since God directed Adam to "sweat to make the soil produce anything."(Genesis 3:19)

An example of soil nutrient depletion comes from a study in China: Chinese farming practices have decreased nitrogen and potassium nutrients within the soil. Only rice crops did not decrease the soils' important nitrogen to phosphorus ratio. The imbalances in nutrients reduce the productivity of the soil. Also, under-compensated farming practices of tractor use, over-tilling and overgrazing have increased the release of carbon from the soil, thereby sending this greenhouse gas into the atmosphere. [1]

What is the problem with such farming practices?   How could you explain to a Chinese farmer the long-term problem with his practices?

Sustainable farming practices have been used all over the world for centuries. Here is an excerpt from an article which gives a good summary:

Environmental sustainability in agriculture means good stewardship of the natural systems and resources that farms rely on. Among other things, this involves:
- Building and maintaining healthy soil
- Managing water wisely
- Minimizing air, water, and climate pollution
- Promoting biodiversity [2]

God also directed Adam in Genesis 3:17b (NIV):
Because of what you have done, the ground will be under a curse. You will have to work hard all your life to make it produce enough food for you.

Would God's charge to Adam lead him to find sustainable practices? Of the listed practices, what do you think Adam used? What would God want humans to do for long-term food production?

Soil Balances Air

5.   The atmosphere of the earth was created by God with a precise balance of gases. (See Lesson 2 - Second Day - Atmosphere)   At the same time God designed animals and humans to breathe out carbon dioxide. In order to keep the atmosphere in balance, God devised ways to absorb this extra carbon. So, vegetation and trees absorb carbon dioxide, then release the oxygen we need. Waters on the earth absorb carbon, and finally, the soil absorbs carbon from plant life.

> Scientists say that more carbon resides in soil than in the atmosphere and all plant life combined; there are 2,500 billion tons of carbon in soil, compared with 800 billion tons in the atmosphere and 560 billion tons in plant and animal life. [3]

Just as the soil absorbs carbon through decaying plant life, it can release the carbon back into the air. Any disturbance of the soil exposes the carbon to the air, sending more greenhouse gas into the air.   Carbon is released from soil through these agricultural practices: tilling, removing crop residue, overusing fertilizers and pesticides and planting a single crop year after year. While growing a garden is beneficial for the atmosphere, these practices may be harmful. If you plant a garden, do you do any of these?

In fall each year I play a balancing act with the garden: I leave all the plants standing long after they are productive, but not so long that it becomes unsightly. Once it approaches that state I gently bend down the dying plants to the ground, then cover them with leaves raked from our yard. I must admit that I was not doing this because of the carbon they would release if I pulled them and discarded them, but simply to enrich the garden soil. So, now I know that this is the best practice! Similarly, I try to leave the greens of bulb plants until they can be folded down to the ground, since this will send nutrients to the bulb and trap the carbon.

Peatlands

6.   As an inquisitive teenager building terrariums for my florist shop job, I investigated the best soils for plants. My findings were put to use in a corner of our garage stacked with clay pots and bags of the soil components. Mom did not seem to mind, since the plants were a nice touch around the house. One of these bags contained "peat," which was intended to help the roots breathe, to improve drainage and to increase nutrient absorption. If you are a gardener, do you add peat to your flower beds and vegetable garden?

My investigations back then told me little about the organic matter, peat. It is plant matter which only partially decays due to excess water and a lack of oxygen. It forms over thousands of years, locking carbon underground in areas of wetlands or of heavy rainfall. Ten percent of freshwater worldwide is found in peatlands, while one third of the world's carbon is held there. In order to harvest the peat for fuel and for agriculture use, the wetlands are drained, then peat is plowed or vacuumed up. This process releases carbon into the atmosphere, plus disturbs the wildlife habitat or the rainforest under which the peat has formed.   Fortunately, peat use for fuel has dramatically decreased due to concern about carbon release.

So, is peat good for the garden? Is the environmental impact of harvesting worth the benefit? Many gardeners now choose alternative materials such as perlite, vermiculite or compost. Here is a good article to guide your choice: " What Every Gardener Should Know About Peat Moss (Plus 5 Alternatives)," by Linsey Knerl, Gardeners Path, July 25, 2017, https://gardenerspath.com/how-to/beginners/peat-moss/. [4] If you use peat to supplement your garden soil, will you continue to do so, or will you look for alternatives?

Permafrost

7.   The Bible speaks of ice in Job 38:29-30:

> From whose womb comes the ice? Who gives birth to the frost from the heavens
> when the waters become hard as stone, when the surface of the deep is frozen?

God is posing these questions to Job. How should Job answer?

There are frigid areas of the earth. Do you think it was God's design to have these cold regions on the earth? Can you guess what may be their purpose?

Did you ever make ice cubes with mint leaves inside? After floating in your lemonade for a bit, the ice has disappeared, and a fresh mint leaf floats along. Permafrost is like this: plant matter, soil, sand and rocks are frozen in ice indefinitely for long term. Unfortunately, warmer temperatures in the colder polar regions have caused thawing of permafrost. (For example, on June 20, 2020, Siberia in the Arctic Circle reached 100.4 degrees F.) As more permafrost thaws, there will be impacts on the planet:

- The carbon stored in the plant matter and the soil will be released into the air. Also, methane, an even more harmful greenhouse gas, may be released.
- Northern villages and roads built on permafrost will break apart and deteriorate.
- Ancient bacteria and viruses locked into the ice from a time many thousands of years ago may be released. Humans certainly do not need another virus after Covid19. [5]

What is God thinking as He looks at the ground He designed to be frozen, turning into slush? Is His original purpose for that land changed?

It may seem like a problem for other people, those residing in the colder climates. However, additional greenhouse gases, carbon and methane, do impact our atmosphere worldwide. Each person can help reduce the warming around the earth, as I have noted in other lessons. Do you believe you can help?

Building on Permafrost

8.   Kids are never happy once the snowman melts, leaving the hat, button eyes, carrot nose and neck scarf on a pile of slushy snow. Sadly, it would be worse to see your house collapse on slushy ice. Or, to have a train wreck because of the melted permafrost under the track.

Building on permafrost becomes a necessity in cold areas of the world, such as Alaska. However, any structure is vulnerable to ground shifts and collapse in warmer temperatures. A first step is drilling to find the depth of the vulnerable area. Steel pilings can be sunk past this depth if possible, then the building constructed on these. If you have seen houses constructed in coastal areas, this is the idea. A small amount of space would be allowed between the ground and the base of the building, to keep the warm building from affecting the permafrost. Further steps would help keep the permafrost frozen: more shade trees, more ground cover plants, etc. Finding a water supply for these buildings must be planned for, since "ground water" would be "ground ice," in the form of permafrost. Then, there is also the question of future temperatures: If the atmosphere continues warming, the permafrost will melt faster, but when will it affect the house? [6]

China hoped to extend transportation and freight movement from its eastern cities over the Tibetan Plateau. The Qinghai-Xizang railroad opened in 2007. Engineers layered crushed rock on the ground to insulate the permafrost, plus elevated the track on bridge-like pilings built deep into the frozen ground. This approach should extend the life of this track on permafrost better than any road or rail construction built directly on the land would. [7]

Have you ever lived in an area built on permafrost? This problem may be outside of your experience, but do you believe we could do anything to help our Canadian neighbors, or the Alaskans?

Erosion

9.   In an effort to demonstrate erosion to my daughter's Girls Scout troop, I brought two plastic containers with two different "landscapes." In one I put in a slope of soil with well-established grass, while in the other I put a slope of barren ground. First the girls poured the sprinkler can of water on the grass-covered slope. Most of the "rain" was absorbed on the grassy slope, with little water accumulating at the bottom. Next the girls poured the sprinkler water on the barren slope. Most of the water ran down, looking quite brown at the bottom. What conclusions did I expect the girls to draw?

I also hoped the girls would extend the idea further than my containers would allow. If the landscape was covered by trees, like a forest, what would happen with heavy rain? What would happen with heavy rain if this forest was cut down for cropland, for cattle grazing land, for lumber or for paper production?

Unfortunately, this scene is not a far-fetched scenario. This happens everyday around the world. When the top layer of soil washes away, the soil quality and, thus, ability to grow crops, is reduced. Also, water quality is affected with sediment, silt and chemical contamination. Do you know of an erosion problem in your area?

Restoration Programs

10. Years of economic development, especially in developing countries, have left much land degraded through poor agricultural and cattle grazing practices. Fortunately in China the Conversion of Cropland to Forest Program has restored more than 28 million hectares (about 20 million football fields) of barren or degraded farmland. This program, also called "Grain for Green," pays farmers to plant trees and restore their land. The abandonment of croplands leaves the long-term benefit questionable if funding ends and farmers have not found other employment. At that point farmers may return to their old farming practices.[8]

How do you feel about initiatives like the Conversion of Cropland to Forest Program?

Desertification

11. Deuteronomy 32:10 speaks of how God cared for man in the desert:
> In a desert land he found him, in a barren and howling waste.   He shielded him and cared for him; he guarded him as the apple of his eye.   (NIV)

In contrast, Jeremiah 17:6 refers to God's treatment of man who turns from Him:

> This is what the Lord says: "Cursed is the one who trusts in man, who draws strength from mere flesh and whose heart turns away from the Lord. That person will be like a bush in the wastelands; they will not see prosperity when it comes. They will dwell in the parched places of the desert, in a salt land where no one lives. (NIV)

How is the desert described in these verses? Compare the way that God's people fare in these two examples.

God's design for the earth included areas of desert. Even though we do not think of cold polar regions having deserts, the Antarctica Desert is the largest.   The second largest is the Sahara Desert, about the size of the continental US. A study of this desert over 93 years showed its expansion by 10 percent, with summer measures showing nearly 16 percent increase. One scientist participating in the study at the University of Maryland, Sumant Nigam explained:

Our results are specific to the Sahara, but they likely have implications for the world's other deserts… The entire Chad Basin falls in the region where the Sahara has crept southward, and the lake is drying out... It's a very visible footprint of reduced rainfall not just locally, but across the whole region. It's an indicator of declining water in the Chad Basin. [9]

Even though the Sahara Desert is probably far from your home, what do you think about its expansion? Do you believe what happens in Africa has any effect on what happens to you? Likewise, do you believe that desertification of the land worldwide happens due to anything you do?

Shrinking Islands

12.   If you do not live on an island or in a coastal area, you probably have no sense of the rise in sea level. Unfortunately, there are numerous populated islands which are at risk.   Isaiah 40:15 speaks of God's view of islands:

> Behold, the nations are like a drop from a bucket,
> And are regarded as a speck of dust on the scales;
> Behold, He lifts up the islands like fine dust.

How does Isaiah describe God's view of nations and islands?   Is this verse simply a comparison of the earth with the immensity of God, or a comment on God's view of islands?

Isaiah 42:10 emphasizes the praises to the Lord which come from the "end of the earth" and the "islands:"

> Sing to the Lord a new song,
> Sing His praise from the end of the earth!
> You who go down to the sea, and all that is in it.
> You islands, and those who dwell on them.

Based on this verse, what would be the purpose of all of the lands and the islands? Does God look at all people on earth as having the same value?

Because of more violent storms and rising sea level, numerous islands are shrinking:

In October 2018, Hurricane Walaka washed away a remote, 11-acre Hawaiian island as the storm barreled through the Pacific Ocean. Several months before that, Russian scientists reported that a small Arctic island had disappeared, saying that only vast, open water remained at the site. And near the end of 2018, a local newspaper reported that an uninhabited islet off the coast of Japan could no longer be found, presumably because it had sunk beneath the water's surface. In these recent examples, the islands were small and uninhabited, but scientists say the fate of these tiny pieces of land could be a harbinger of what's to come. [10]

How do you believe God feels about islands shrinking? What if an inhabited island faces this potential risk, what should the people do who are living there?

Shrinking Coastlines

13. Indonesia is moving its capital city. The large population in Jakarta has extracted so much groundwater, that the ground level and surface water resources have been impacted. Add to that the storms and rising sea level to yield the sinking city of Jakarta with half of its area below sea level. . In August of 2019 President Joko Widodo announced the move of the capital to the rain forest area of Borneo. [11]   Should coastal cities which have been inundated with flooding and storms move inland?

Another island which is battling sea level rise is Kiribati in the Pacific Ocean, between Australia and Hawaii. Rising sea level, increasing salinity of water supplies and increased vulnerability to disasters have prompted leaders to consider options. Their preceding president, Tong, purchased land in Fuji with the plan to move the homeland. His successor as of June 2020, Maamua, is now embarking on a dredging campaign to raise the level of the three islands. Part of his plan is to remove the causeways and replace these with an elevated roadway connecting the islands. These plans include a political component with rival interests for the islands represented by the US and China. [12]

How do you believe a shrinking coastline or shrinking island be dealt with? Do you believe that competing countries with political interests should have a voice?   In reality, what do you think might happen to Kiribati?

Avalanches

14.   Have you ever seen an avalanche? I hope that you have never been in one. God speaks to the snow in Job 37:6-7:

> He says to the snow, 'Fall on the earth,' and to the rain shower, 'Be a mighty downpour. So that everyone he has made may know his work, he stops all people from their labor.

Based on the verses in Job, what is God's purpose in snow?   Unfortunately, sometimes the snow does "fall on the earth" in the form of an avalanche. Do you think avalanches are in God's design for the earth?

The Bible speaks of the Proverbs 31 woman in verse 21:

> She is not afraid of snow for her household, For all her household is clothed with scarlet.

What do you think Proverbs 31:21 is saying about this woman? Do you think there is any direction here for humans who try to anticipate and predict avalanches? Would this verse have application to avalanches?

Scientists do try to predict avalanches. There are several impetuses for avalanches: heavier snow increases magnitude, warmer temperatures make layers unstable, or rain-on-snow destabilizes layers. When the risk is high, transportation personnel try to reduce it by closing roads and triggering avalanches, in other words, trying to beat it at its game.   However, in 2019 the experts were surprised, with 346 avalanches reported in Colorado during the week of March 8th. The preceding weather probably contributed: the three months preceding were the wettest winter on record in the contiguous USA.

With global warming, warmer air absorbs more moisture, resulting in more precipitation, which in turn may cause more avalanches worldwide. In 2019 avalanches killed skiers in New Mexico, closed roads in California and Utah, and trapped thousands of people in the European Alps. You may say, "This is a known risk for ski vacationers." However, in addition to the loss of property and life, road blockages due to avalanches affect transport of goods and people. [13]

What could we do to reduce the number of avalanches around the world?

Conclude and Respond

Imagine how difficult it is to live in an area of frequent flooding, such as Miami or Jakarta. After hurricane Sandy hit the northeastern US I recall seeing dumpsters filled with wallboard, carpets and possessions. Often the entire first floor of a home had to be "removed" because of the water damage. Such an experience would be stressful, if not traumatic. No wonder the estimates of damage every time there is a hurricane in the US are so high.

This week think about the people in Indonesia, Kiribiti and coastal areas of frequent flooding like Miami. Pray that God would guide their government leaders regarding the best action. Also pray that people around the world would take action to help with problems such as melting permafrost and sea level rise.

Lesson 4 – Action Steps
- Support organic farmers by buying their products.
- Do not use peat on garden; alternatives are compost and coconut coir.
- Write to lawmakers in support of developing countries' expenses to fight climate change as per agreements in the Glasgow Climate Conference (COP26).

---

[1]   "Agricultural Land Use Decouples Soil Nutrient Cycles in a Subtropical Riparian Wetland in China," prepared by CATENA, ScienceDirect, October 2015,, https://www.sciencedirect.com/science/article/abs/pii/S0341816215300114

[2] "What is Sustainable Agriculture?" prepared by Union of Concerned Scientists, April 10, 2017, https://www.ucsusa.org/resources/what-sustainable-agriculture

[3]   Judith Schwartz, "Soil as Carbon Storehouse: New Weapon in Climate Fight?" prepared by Yale University, March 4, 2014,   https://e360.yale.edu/features/soil_as_carbon_storehouse_new_weapon_in_climate_fight)

[4]   Linsey Knerl, " What Every Gardener Should Know About Peat Moss (Plus 5 Alternatives),"   Gardeners Path, July 25, 2017, https://gardenerspath.com/how-to/beginners/peat-moss/

[5]   "What Is Permafrost?" prepared by NASA Climate Kids, accessed August 2020, https://climatekids.nasa.gov/permafrost/#:~:text=and%20South%20Poles.-,Permafrost%20is%20any%20ground%20that%20remains%20completely%20frozen%E2%80%9432%C2%B0,large%20regions%20of%20the%20Earth.

[6] Ravena Koenig, "In Fairbanks, Building a Home on Permafrost Is Tricky," AP News, October 6, 2018, https://apnews.com/a3e0b1b176dc454b9cfb8fbc512219c9/In-Fairbanks,-building-a-home-on-permafrost-is-tricky#:~:text=Basically%2C%20Benesch's%20house%20is%20built,to%20water%20when%20it%20thaws.&text=That's%20a%20Fairbanks%2Dbased%20nonprofit,environments%20and%20provides%20public%20education.)

[7]   "'People and Frozen Ground," prepared by National Snow and Ice Data Center, University of Colorado Boulder, accessed July 2020, https://nsidc.org/cryosphere/frozenground/people.html

[8]   Qi Zhang, et al., "Divergent socioeconomic-ecological outcomes of China's conversion of cropland to forest program in the subtropical mountainous area and the semi-arid Loess Plateau," Science Direct, October 2020, https://www.sciencedirect.com/science/article/pii/S2212041620301091#s0050

[9]   Cheryl Dybas and Matt Wright, " New Study Finds World's Largest Desert, the Sahara, Has Grown By 10 Percent Since 1920," National Science Foundation, News Release 18-018, March 29, 2018, https://www.nsf.gov/news/news_summ.jsp?cntn_id=244804

[10] Denise Chow, "Three Islands Disappeared in the Past Year. Is Climate Change to Blame?" prepared by NBC News, June 9, 2019, https://www.nbcnews.com/mach/science/three-islands-disappeared-past-year-climate-change-blame-ncna1015316

[11]   Bill Chappell, "Jakarta Is Crowded And Sinking, So Indonesia Is Moving Its Capital To Borneo," National Public Radio, August 26, 2019, https://www.npr.org/2019/08/26/754291131/indonesia-plans-to-move-capital-to-borneo-from-jakarta#:~:text=Asia-,Jakarta%20Is%20Crowded%20And%20Sinking%2C%20So%20Indonesia,Moving%20Its%20Capital%20To%20Borneo&text=AFP%2FGetty%20Images-,Indonesian%20President%20Joko%20Widodo%20(center)%20says%20the%20new%20capital%20city,on%20the%20island%20of%20Borneo.&text=The%20capital's%20current%20location%20faces,the%20fact%20that%20it's%20sinking.

[12]   Christopher Pala, "Kiribati's President's Plans to Raise Islands in Fight Against Sea-Level Rise," by Christopher Pala, The Guardian, August 9, 2020, https://www.theguardian.com/world/2020/aug/10/kiribatis-presidents-plans-to-raise-islands-in-fight-against-sea-level-rise

[13]   Bob Berwyn, "Avalanches Menace Colorado as Climate Change Raises the Risk," Insideclimate News, March 9, 2019, https://insideclimatenews.org/news/08032019/avalanche-climate-change-risk-snow-storm-forecast-colorado-switzerland

Lesson 5 - God's Vision of the Earth on the Third Day: Vegetation (Part 1)

Have you ever visited an arboretum or a garden exhibition? The National Arboretum in Washington, DC, is an amazing display, as is Longwood Gardens in Pennsylvania, or the Palmengarten in Frankfurt, Germany. The beauty in the variety of plants displayed is another testament to God's great work.   Although I have never seen a rainforest in person, I have been in representations of them at these arboretums. The feeling is one of harmony and vitality. These thriving gardens depict for me what I think is God's vision of vegetation on the earth. Have you ever been in a rainforest? If so, what was your impression of it?

1. The Bible mentions God's handiwork in the following verses. Describe His purposes for trees and vegetation as described in each.

      1Chronicles 16:33 a

      Acts 14:17

      Song of Solomon 2:12

      Isaiah 32:15-16

2.   In Genesis 1:11(ESV) God commanded the Earth to "sprout vegetation, plants yielding seeds and fruit trees bearing fruit which is their seed."   In order for the Earth to "sprout forth," the land must be able to nourish the vegetation. In addition, water must be available, as described in Ezekiel 47:12:

>   And on the banks, on both sides of the river, there will grow all kinds of trees for food. Their leaves will not wither, nor their fruit fail, but they will bear fresh fruit every month, because the water for them flows from the sanctuary. Their fruit will be for food, and their leaves for healing.

Think about the variety of plants and fruit which God has designed. Choose your favorite type of fruit and/or vegetable. Describe what is necessary to cultivate it to yield "fruit" and "seed."

3.   In my backyard there is a small area which is in its natural "forest" stage.   There are numerous trees of varying size and variety. The forest floor is covered with decaying leaves, rotting tree branches and a variety of native underbrush. We do nothing to help or hurt this environment other than seasonally adding more leaves raked from our yard. As I see the plants, trees, birds and animals thriving there, I can imagine what this part of earth once looked like.

Notice that God designed the vegetation and trees to produce seeds. Thus, his design allowed for the vegetation and trees to continue to cover the earth forever. Can you name an area that still looks like it did when God designed it?

4.   These are some situations in the Bible where God's retribution for people's actions came in the form of destruction of fertile land. As you read these verses, make note of the actions of God's people and God's response:
Nehemiah 9:35

Isaiah 10:12 and 18

Jeremiah 2:7

How do you imagine God feels about man's actions?

Seeds

5.   Read these two Bible passages and make note of what God says about seed:

Mark 4:3-8

Genesis 1:29-30

How did God design every plant?   For what purpose did He do this?

The second passage is actually a parable about God's word going out to receptive people rather than literally about seed growth. Still it does reflect what happens to seeds when they fall on poor ground. Years ago my daughter did her science project on plant growth in various soils. From the Mark passage, you could guess that her plants growing in the rocky soil and the overly sandy soil did not prosper, while her plant in the potting soil mix grew well. If you are a gardener, how do you assure good quality soil for your plants?

Trees and the Atmosphere

6.   Understanding how trees and plants live reveals another of God's amazing designs! Trees and plants use carbon dioxide, sunlight and water to grow. Do you remember what this process is called? Yes, photosynthesis. In the photosynthesis process trees breathe out oxygen, which is exactly what humans need. Humans breathe in the oxygen, and they breathe out carbon dioxide, which is exactly what trees and plants need. Yes, you are clever God!

The bible verses above show that plants and trees provide beauty, food and healing. Add to this list the absorption of carbon dioxide, followed by the release of oxygen. But, our omniscient God went a step further. Remember from the "Atmosphere" section how God designed the air so that life could thrive? God made a precise balance of gases, at the best temperatures for all life. Trees and plants assist in balancing the gases, by absorbing carbon dioxide in the air.   It follows that with fewer trees than God originally planned, their carbon-absorbing results are diminished.

True, tree-planting efforts in the last 35 years have helped to replace trees removed by human activity. However, this quote from "Fact Check: Are There Really More Trees Today Than 100 Years Ago?" explains where we stand:

> Today, annual tree harvest vs. production on a world-wide scale shows that humans cut down approximately 15 billion trees a year and re-plant about 5 billion. That's a net loss of 10 billion trees every year, and a rate that would mean the loss of all trees within the next 300 years. [1]

Numbers are not the whole story. Maintaining the balance as God planned for the tree-absorption of carbon dioxide depends on having trees with the same capability. An 800-year old redwood tree will absorb much more carbon dioxide than a one-year old redwood seedling. Also, since tropical forests provide components of medicines, the loss of a tree from a tropical forest is likely greater than the loss of a tree in my backyard. Do you have trees in your yard? Have you cut down any trees in your yard or lost any through storm damage?   Have you planted any trees in your yard and watched their growth year after year?

Trees: Sink or Sunk?

7.   If trees and plants are burned or fallen and decomposed, the carbon is released into the air. However, if trees and plants continue to grow, or are made into a wood product, the carbon is SUNK. This means it will stay in the tree or the wood product. So, if trees are cut down, made into lumber, then used to build a home, the carbon is locked into that home forever if it is not salvaged or burned. How much of your home, including furniture and flooring, is made of wood? What would be a good way to dispose of used wooden furniture?

Similarly, when paper is made from trees, the carbon is locked into that paper until the paper is thrown in the trash. Disposed paper holds carbon for two to three years, whereas newsprint holds it a little longer. Once in the landfill it may be released as methane, which is a more potent greenhouse gas. The best disposal for paper is recycling. [2] Do you recycle paper and junk mail from your home and/or business?

Another one of my quirky habits is that I cut off the secure info on documents when I place the paper into recycling. The "un-quirky" way to handle secure documents is shredding. Do you shred your documents?

Besides using electric power for this machine, people often put the shredded material into the trash, where it decomposes and releases carbon and methane into the air. However, this is what you could do:

- Find out whether your town accepts the shredded paper and the special handling steps.
- Donate to a pet shelter for bedding.
- Cut off or cross out with permanent marker the secure info, then recycle.

Knowing this info about paper, will you change your approach?

Wildfires

8.   In recent years in the United States the news is frequently marked with forest fires scenes. One of the most chilling scenes I recall was of the gridlock traffic becoming engulfed by the flames as hopeless souls in the cars waited for the end. It is hard to imagine that wildfires were ever part of God's design.

These verses give us a view of God's purpose for fire. Read them and make note of the purpose:

Mark 14:54

John 21:9

The following verses describe very different uses of fire. Read these and name each use:

Matthew 3:11

Luke 9:54

Acts 2:3

I find the verse Exodus 22:6 very interesting:

> If a fire breaks out and spreads into thorn bushes so that it burns shocks of grain or standing grain or the whole field, the one who started the fire must make restitution.

Three California utilities have been dealing with the liability from deadly wildfires in 2018. Do you think the source of wildfires should be tracked, and be financially responsible for the losses?

Read this passage about fire at the end of the age: Matthew 13:37-40.   This verse depicts the weeds, which are "the people of the evil one," being burned at the end. Some Christians believe that some of the current environmental destruction, such as wildfires, are simply signs of the end of the age. How do you feel about this? Do you believe God will be giving us signs?

Wildfires Worldwide

9.   These are the top six countries around the world which have had the most wildfires in 2019: Congo, Russia, Australia, Brazil, Angola and Mozambique. Unless you regularly study this concern, you were probably surprised by some of this list. [3]

Congo - While the African (Congo, Angola, Mozambique) fires are usually smaller and in savannah areas which rejuvenate rapidly for the next growing season, some have been set by farmers for clearing in the rainforest areas of the Congo Basin. Mozambique has been losing over 285,000 hectares to forest fires annually. (Each hectare is an area of nearly 2 football fields. So, 285,000 hectares would be about 570,000 football fields...annually!) These governments realize the need to better educate the farmers about the importance of the rainforest. [4]

Russia - In Siberia, Russia, the early and unusually hot summer has precipitated more and wide-reaching forest fires. About half of the forests in Russia are in remote areas, where firefighters are instructed to avoid unless buildings or lives are threatened. Thus, the fires there burn on, turning carbon sinking forests into carbon-emitters. [5]

Australia - 2019 brought perfect conditions for an intense fire season in Australia: the year was the hottest and driest on record, with a national average temperature record of 107.4 degrees Fahrenheit on December 18. The wildfires in summer 2019/2020 left Australia with the loss of one billion animals, 33 people, 3000 homes and an area the size of South Korea burned. The smoke and ashes created an air quality index 23 times higher than "hazardous." Australia's distinct conditions allow it to host 244 unique species, which have been subject to the highest extinction rate worldwide for mammals over the past 200 years. [6]

Brazil - Clearing and fires in the Brazilian rainforest increased after the election of President Jair Bolsonaro, due to his policies of reduced fines. Images of intense widespread burning in the Amazon attracted international attention in August of 2019, when the G7 nations offered immediate logistical and financial support to fight the fires. However, this offer was rejected by Bolsonaro, despite his acceptance of help from Israel and Chile. The fires, while releasing large amounts of the greenhouse gas carbon dioxide, have also sent the toxic gas, carbon monoxide, along the coasts of South America.   Although the fires are controlled in the rainy season, the figures for June 2020 already show 20 percent increase over previous years. [7]   Add to that the extent of deforestation in January 2020: an area 83 times New York City's Central Park, which is double the measure from one year before. [8]

Arizona, USA - In the United States Arizona is in the midst of a terrible fire season (July 2020), due to extreme heat and drought, with three of its current fires ranking in the all-time top ten for AZ. Generally pollution in the form of smoke and ash is a concern. However, this year there is additional concern, especially in light of higher coronavirus case numbers in Arizona:

Recent scientific studies examining England and Italy have linked Covid-19 morbidity to poor air quality of the likes yielded by wildfire smoke. [9]

10.   What is wrong with wildfires (other than the obvious)? If you live near forested areas, the image of "controlled burning" may come to mind. Forest management staff will periodically set and monitor fires in the ground level vegetation, with the goal of reducing widespread fires. Science supports this approach, even though fires may still break out. Have you seen controlled burning near you?

During August and September of 2020 the western states of the United States have seen extensive fires. While inadequate clearing of the ground level vegetation may be contributing, the unusually hot and dry weather creates a tinderbox ready to catch fire. Also, the spruce budworm attacks the evergreen trees there, leaving them in a combustible state. The weather extremes have also generated lightning flashes without rain, serving as the needed spark. Firefighters talk about never-seen-before fire movement: the fire jumps along the tops of trees rather than the common path of movement along the ground. A plan to reduce the number and extent of the fires must cover all bases.

Here are the potential consequences of wildfires:
- Death of humans, animals, birds, insects.
- Destruction of homes, businesses, forests and habitats.
- Far-reaching smoke clouds of carbon dioxide, particles and harmful gases (carbon monoxide and other toxic gases).
- Dangerous local air quality.
- Emission of carbon by trees as opposed to absorption of carbon by trees.
- Loss of biodiversity

Were you aware of the extent of wildfires worldwide? Is there anything each of us can do to help reduce these?

As with many of the issues I have introduced, since in most cases the fires are more widespread due to higher temperatures and more drought, each of us can take steps to reduce our carbon footprint/greenhouse gas emissions. The Brazilian situation was exacerbated by the president's policies, so one active step is to vote for politicians who favor good environmental policies. Do you consider environmental policies when you vote?

Deforestation

11.   If you have had the opportunity to walk through a forest on a sunny day, you could certainly understand the depiction of 1 Chronicles 16:33:

> Let the trees of the forest sing, let them sing for joy before the Lord…

Describe your experience(s) with the beauty of the God's forests.

Another view of God's design of forests is found in Psalm 29. After verse 1 emphasizes the Lord's glory and strength, verse 5 and 9 describe God's handling of the forests:

> Ascribe to the Lord, you heavenly beings, ascribe to the Lord glory and strength. (1)
> The voice of the Lord breaks the cedars; the Lord breaks in pieces the cedars of Lebanon.(5)
> The voice of the Lord twists the oaks and strips the forests bare. (9)

What did the Psalmist mean in describing this destructive scene? Would God do this today? What does God think of humans destroying forests?

Fortunately, there are watchdog agencies such as the Forest Stewardship Council to monitor forest-use practices. This council also certifies forest products for their different levels of sustainability: 100% sustainable, 100% recycled materials, or "Mix of these." [10] How do you feel about such agencies monitoring sustainability practices?

Reforestation

12.   A friend of ours reported that he was having some trees cut down on his property for various reasons. He proudly went on to say that he always plants a new tree for each he cuts down. His response is good in that he recognizes the importance of trees, however his action was not equivalent in that the new trees would be a fraction of the size of the cut 80-year old oak trees.

China's valuable resource of the Yellow River Basin reached a tipping point with a 267 day drought in 1997, followed by massive floods in 1998 which destroyed over 13 million homes and killed 3600 people. This happened because many years of rapid development left the country with severe loss of forest and erosion of sloping farmlands. In 1999 the government implemented programs to address this problem: the Conversion of Cropland to Forest Program and the National Forest Protection Program.   Besides remedying the land and forest problems, the programs were designed to help local farmers with compensation for their loss of farmland. Environmental results have been somewhat better than economic results. [11]

The Bonn Challenge forest restoration program was initiated in 2011 between the International Union for Conservation of Nature (IUCN) and Germany. Their first goal year, 2020, set the target of 150 million hectares pledged for planting. The results exceeded this, with 210 million hectares pledged. Actual results may fall below this, in part because of the extent of forest fires: as of April 2020, fire alerts worldwide were up 13% compared to the high incidence of alerts in 2019. [12] Through this program:

Related forest landscape restoration programs in 40 countries created 354,000 long- and short-term jobs. The program highlighted restoration's importance across sectors, including in agriculture, energy, water, poverty alleviation and climate change.   They also sequestered 1.379 billion tons of carbon dioxide and generated an average investment per hectare of at least $ 235. [13]

Several of the reforestation programs attempt to address local economies as well as the ill effects of deforestation. Do you believe these are connected?   How would reforestation help the local people?

Local Tree Clearing

13.   Other human activities, such as urban/suburban sprawl, require the clearing of trees. Several years ago my husband and I were house-hunting in nearby communities. In one community it was obvious that the new houses had been built with little disruption to existing landscape. That town's code reads:

> An owner or developer shall remove only such trees, vegetation and underbrush as is necessary to construct and install the structure and improvements authorized by the Planning Board or Board of Adjustment. All sites should be developed, to the extent possible, in a manner which will result in the least amount of disturbance to the natural site. [14]

In addition, that town has clearly specified rules for tree removal by homeowners or businesses. Hooray! Are there any local ordinances limiting tree removal in your town? Why do people want to remove healthy trees? Should there be restrictions?

I was dismayed to see a huge area of our local state park cleared one year ago. A park ranger told me that 25 acres of 70-year old cedar trees were cleared because of their susceptibility to damage from large storms. In their place over 1000 tree seedlings were planted, including some planted and monitored by school children. While I am happy about the plantings, I contend that it will take 70 years until these replacements are as effective at absorbing carbon from the atmosphere as their predecessors. In such a situation why not clear the fallen trees, then plant new seedlings among the standing trees?

Mushrooms

14. Do you like mushrooms? God designed these as a "wonder plant." These are the health benefits: :

- They have cancer-fighting properties for breast cancer and prostate cancer. Plus, lentinan from shiitake mushrooms boosts the immune system for slowing cancer cell growth.
- Beta-glucan and lentinan from mushrooms are immunity-boosters.
- Their phytonutrients help lower cholesterol by keeping cells from sticking in blood vessels and forming plaque.
- Mushrooms are one of the few food sources for vitamin D; while crimini mushrooms are high in B12. .
- Reishi mushrooms have anti-inflammatory powers to fight disease, suppress allergic reactions, reduce tumor growth and lower inflammation.
- A psychedelic compound, psilocybin, found in basidiomycota mushrooms, helped cancer patients with depression, anxiety or fear of death.
- Many mushrooms, but primarily porcini mushrooms, are high in two antioxidants associated with anti-aging properties. [15]

Mushrooms are an environmental "cure all" in that they detoxify the soil, and they can clean up oil spills. Psychedelic mushrooms can be used to treat alcoholism, cancer and PTSD (Post Traumatic Stress Disorder).[16] God locked all of these secrets into mushrooms! Did you know of any of these health benefits for mushrooms? Do you intend to use mushrooms more often in your cooking after reading this?

Conclude and Respond

It is easy to think about wildfires in the western United States, in Russia, in the Amazon, in Australia, etc., as regional problems. Do you believe these are a bigger problem? Even though controlled forest fires could be beneficial for the prevention of future fires, it is hard to believe that God wants massive fires like those happening now. Consider whether you believe man has a role in the fires. Pray that God would show you if there is something you can do to help.

Lesson 5 – Action Steps
- Recycle ALL paper by blacking out or cutting off account numbers. Determine if shredded paper can be delivered to separate government facilities.
- Plant more trees in your yard/your community. Avoid cutting down trees; if necessary, plant 3-4 new trees in place of one larger tree.
- Ask local officials to institute better policies for tree clearing for building projects.

[1] the environmentor, "Fact Check: Are There Really More Trees Today Than 100 Years Ago?", tentree.com, October 22, 2017, https://www.tentree.com/blogs/posts/fact-check-are-there-really-more-trees-today-than-100-years-ago#:~:text=We%20had%20rudimentary%20estimates%20based,good%20or%20well%2Ddocumented%20science.

[2] Jialu Chen, "Does Using Paper Take CO2 Out of the Environment ?" Mother Jones, April 4, 2012, https://www.motherjones.com/environment/2012/04/paper-carbon-dioxide-sequester/

[3] "Global Forest Watch - Fires," prepared by globalforestwatch.org, accessed July 2020, https://fires.globalforestwatch.org/report/index.html#aoitype=ALL&reporttype=globalcountryreport&dates=fYear-2019!fMonth-7!fDay-7!tYear-2020!tMonth-7!tDay-6)

[4] Kossivi Tiassou, "Amazon versus Africa forest fires: Is the world really ablaze?" , Prepared by Deustche Welle, accessed July 2020, (https://www.dw.com/en/amazon-versus-africa-forest-fires-is-the-world-really-ablaze/a-50229553

[5] Alejandra Borunda, "What a 100-Degree Day in Siberia Really Means, National Geographic, June 23, 2020, https://www.nationalgeographic.com/science/2020/06/what-100-degree-day-siberia-means-climate-change/

[6] Justine Calma, "What You Need to Know About the Australia Bushfires," The Verge, February 13, 2020, https://www.theverge.com/2020/1/3/21048891/australia-wildfires-koalas-climate-change-bushfires-deaths-animals-damage)

[7] The Visual and Data Journalism Team, "Amazon Fires at 13-Year High for June," BBC News, July 2, 2020, https://www.bbc.com/news/world-latin-america-49433767)

[8] Rhett A. Butler, "Deforestation in Brazil Continues Torrid Pace into 2020," Mongabay Series, February 9, 2020, https://news.mongabay.com/2020/02/deforestation-in-brazil-continues-torrid-pace-into-2020/)

[9] Steve Horn, "Arizona Reels as Three of the Biggest Wildfires in its History Ravage State," The Guardian, July 2, 2020, https://www.theguardian.com/environment/2020/jul/02/arizona-wildfires)

[10] Forest Stewardship Council, https://fsc.org/en

[11] Lucas Gutiérrez Rodríguez, Nicholas J. Hogarth, Wen Zhou, Chen Xie, Kun Zhang & Louis Putzel, "China's Conversion of Cropland to Forest Program: a Systematic Review of the Environmental and Socioeconomic Effects," Environmental Evidence Journal, Article number: 21 (2016), September 12, 2016, https://environmentalevidencejournal.biomedcentral.com/articles/10.1186/s13750-016-0071-x#ref-CR10

[12] James Petts, "2020 is the First Bonn Challenge Deadline. What Does the Barometer Say?," September 1, 2020, https://news.globallandscapesforum.org/38040/2020-is-the-first-bonn-challenge-deadline-what-does-the-barometer-say/

[13] "Restore Our Future: The Bonn Challenge, " prepared by International Union for Conservation of Nature, accessed June 2020, https://www.bonnchallenge.org/content/challenge)

[14] "130-52 Selective Clearing," Prepared by Township of Stafford, NJ, accessed June 2020, https://ecode360.com/11376158

[15] Angela Nelson, "7 Surprising Health Benefits of Mushrooms," Treehugger.com, January 22, 2020, https://www.treehugger.com/surprising-health-benefits-mushrooms-4864212)

[16] Wendy Becktold, "Much Ado About Mushrooms," Sierra Magazine, May/June 2020

Lesson 6 - God's Vision of the Earth on the Third Day: Vegetation (Part 2)

What is your favorite flower? Did you know that there are about 369,000 species of flowering plants?   So, I understand if you cannot decide on your favorite. This, again, shows how amazing God is. Not only has He designed beautiful, colorful, unique flowers, but about 17,000 species are used as medicine. Sadly, 21% of the flowering plants are threatened with extinction. [1] Rainforest clearing for cattle ranching to produce beef is one of the biggest threats, with global warming also contributing.   If so many flowers are lost forever, our earth will certainly be changed from what God planned.

1. Not only did God create vegetation, but He created it "according to its kind." Read Genesis 1:11-13.

Thus, He created many kinds of plants and trees. Each of these kinds was designed to thrive in a specific climate, in a specific area on earth. This lesson presents several of these species, including the recent challenges for each.

2. Locked in many plants and trees on the earth are secrets of great value to man. Read this verse to find one of the God-designed benefits for vegetation, Revelations 22:2.

> On each side of the river stood the tree of life, bearing twelve crops of fruit, yielding its fruit every month. And the leaves of the tree are for the healing of the nations.

What is this extra benefit of vegetation?

Did you ever hear of a cloud forest?

3. Cloud forests are a type of rainforest in the higher, cooler elevations of the tropics. Their name comes from the misty, cloud-like humid air enveloping them, enabling trees, plants, ferns and lichens to grow in a mountainous region. Because of being in higher elevations with rocky soil, trees will be short, twisted and covered with mosses and lichens. God's ingenious design allows these forests to provide up to 75% of the water in the high-elevation streams, which in turn feed the rivers of the area. God knew what he was doing, because these forests have enabled inhabitants of the lower lands to flourish.

Want an example of man messing with God's design? On the island of Anujuan off the east coast of Africa farmers have been clearing these forests for farmland since the 1950s. With the cloud forests disappearing, the mountain streams are shrinking, and the rivers are no longer meeting the water and irrigation needs of the inhabitants. Farmers have resorted to using chemical fertilizers, which causes other problems. Dry season no longer allows sufficient water for supporting population growth on the island. Thus, tens of thousands have sought other occupations, or migrated to neighboring islands. Some help is coming from the non-profit Dahari in reforesting some of the hardest hit areas. [2]

Unfortunately, this one example is representative of what is happening in many developing areas of the world.

Do you believe rich countries should try to help in situations like this? Do you think that there is any way you personally could help?

Cedars of Lebanon

4.   From the time that my children were young, the family would hike in a nearby park which centered around "Cedar Creek." Fortunately there was a huge cedar tree in the yard where I grew up, so I could easily identify the cedars in the park where we hiked. One section was dominated by these, separated by a reverent path where even the children walked in silence. I like to think of cedars as having the best posture, or perhaps as being the most regal of all trees. There is also the distinct "treasure chest" smell of cedar, which I had the good fortune of finding in my bedroom closet at one place I lived, and later in a second hand cedar chest I acquired. Have you ever walked in a cedar forest, or seen a cedar tree?   Do you have a cedar chest?

The country of Lebanon is famous for its cedar forests, as it was in Bible times. Here are a few references about the cedars of Lebanon. Read these and note the descriptions of the cedar trees.
Psalm 92:13

Song of Solomon 5:15

1 KIngs 7:2

Unfortunately the cedars have not fared well, even in Biblical times when trees were harvested for building projects or fuel. Through the years the trees have been both harvested and protected, depending on the state of government or warring parties. In the 1960s and 1970s Lebanon's Green Plan directed the planting of numerous cedar seedlings, only to be disbanded during the subsequent civil war.   Fortunately in December 2014 a new reforestation project was initiated with the goal of planting 40 million trees.[3]

As with most tree seedlings, this project's benefit will not be realized for many years. Cedar seedlings will not bear cones for 40 years, and will not reach their stately appearance for close to 100 years. Unfortunately, Lebanon's dispute in June of 2020 with Israel has exposed a political vulnerability of some of the trees: Israel claims that cedar trees next to their concrete border wall will block their critical security views. [4]

How do you feel about Lebanon's commitment to planting more cedars? Do you feel that Israel "has a case" against Lebanon's trees at the border?

Boreal Forests

5.   Picture an endless span of evergreen trees, home to numerous bird and animal species. These boreal forests dominate the lands encircling the Arctic Circle. Boreal Forests store more carbon per hectare than any other type of forest on earth. In fact, if you total all such forests, they hold more carbon than the total of all currently available oil, gas and coal reserves.   Unfortunately, the Canadian boreal forest has lost 28 million acres, the size of Ohio, from 1996 to 2015. Ninety percent of this logging has been "clear cutting," meaning the forests have been totally cleared.

> Every year, the Canadian boreal region, including peatlands, removes carbon dioxide equivalent to the annual emissions of 24 million passenger vehicles. [5]
> Canada ranks third globally in intact forest loss, behind only Russia and Brazil, accounting for 15 percent of the world's intact forest loss between 2000 and 2013. [6]

The spruce and coniferous trees of the boreal forests are coveted for a unique attribute of their softwood pulp: Its longer fibres strengthen paper products, and, thus, mean an enduring demand. What could be done to reduce the loss of the boreal forests?   How could the logging companies be persuaded to use more sustainable practices?

African Forests

6.   Look at the satellite image of Africa on the internet. You will notice how the central equatorial area is covered by greenery, whereas the north and south are both covered by land which is mostly desert. Many of these forested areas have been ravaged for economic benefit. According to the UN Food and Agriculture Organization, African forests are cut down at twice the world's average rate. Translate this deforestation to the increase of greenhouse gases, and alarms bells go off.   Some of the trees are used for local cooking, shelter and heating needs. Some forests are cleared for agriculture. Both of these purposes relate to the population growth demands. Also, the African forests supply medicines for most local populations, since cash and pharmacies are not common. [7]

Do you see a long-term solution for sustaining population growth without further environmental degradation?   What would God want these local people to do? What would God want the governments to do?

Senegal first announced suspension of logging permits in May of 2015, then reiterated the policy in 2018. Unfortunately, insufficient enforcement yielded extensive illegal logging.   This forest region is shared by Gambia, which allowed extensive deforestation under the former president. Local needs are not the primary driver for the timber: the rosewood and mahogany are in high demand in the

Chinese market, with Gambia being the second largest exporter (after Nigeria). How could economic needs be balanced with environmental sustainability? [8]

The African country of Kenya is a major exporter of tea. Forests there help to regulate the correct climate by maintaining humidity and more moderate temperatures for optimum tea growth. The trees prevent erosion by wind and water.   Another reason that Kenya's forests should not be cleared pertains to the cloud forests described in number (3) above. The cloud forests in the mountains replenish the streams, sending water down to the hydroelectric power dams. Kenya relies on hydropower for 70% of its power.   When these forests are cleared, the water flow and power generation decreases. [9]

Another aspect of the African problem is the greed of leaders and local landowners. Illegal land agreements are settled regularly, adding to other causes noted above. Perhaps the way that people in other countries can help is (a) support organizations who are working to educate the locals and improve the situation, and (b) pay attention to their local governments to be sure that wise actions are pursued.

Do you know what your local ordinances are about tree clearing?   Have you ever supported organizations such as the World Wildlife Fund, Audubon, or The Sierra Club?

Clearing the Amazon Rainforest

7.   In the August of 2019 the world was alarmed at the extent of fires in the Amazon rainforest. Perhaps this situation was due to the new Brazilian President Jair Bolsonaro who encouraged tree-clearing activities for economic development. As of July 2019, satellite data revealed that an area the size of a football field was being cleared every minute. However, the extent of the fires was actually worse in the 2000s, with 2005 being the worst year on record. [10]

Quite often these fires are set after a forest has been felled, to further clear the land for cattle or agriculture. Unfortunately, the worldwide demand for beef promotes cattle ranching and the necessary crop production to support the cattle. Do you eat beef?   Did you know that the Amazon Rainforest is being cleared for beef cattle?

Medicinal Rainforest Plants

8.   Plants were used for medicinal purposes in Bible times. Read 2 Kings 20:17:
>   Then Isaiah said, "Prepare a poultice of figs." They did so and applied it to the boil, and he recovered.

Read also Ezekial 47:12:
>   And on the banks, on both sides of the river, there will grow all kinds of trees for food. Their leaves will not wither, nor their fruit fail, but they will bear fresh fruit every month, because the water for them flows from the sanctuary. Their fruit will be for food, and their leaves for healing.

Consider diseases that God has allowed humans to have. From these bible verses, God has also given us cures from plants. What role does God play in helping man find these hidden remedies?

9.   Genesis 2:15 refers to the sixth day of creation when God created man to tend the Garden of Eden:

The Lord God took the man and put him in the Garden of Eden to work it and keep it.

Even though man messed up the opportunity to have the Garden of Eden by eating from the forbidden tree, God still directed man to work the land. With what you know about rainforests, do you believe that the Garden of Eden was at all similar?   What command do you think God would give us now about the rainforests?

10.   There has been worldwide concern in recent years about rainforest destruction through clearing and fires. A regrettable effect of rainforest loss is the loss of medicinal plants. Did you know that seventy percent of plants with cancer-fighting properties exist only in the Amazon rainforest? Most Americans have no idea about the source of medicines they know by the common drug names. The Lapacho plant has been used for cancer treatment, chemotherapy pain relief and to fight infections. Tawari Tree Bark has these same uses, plus is used for treatment of inflammation. Smokers and alcoholics can use the Sodo plant to fight those addictions. And yet another is Pusangade Motelo which provides a natural remedy for anxiety. [11]

The Madagascar rainforest hosts the Rosy Periwinkle from which we have two cancer-fighting drugs: one that treats childhood leukemia, and one that treats Hodgkins' disease. [12] Unknown remedies are still locked in the plants under threat of clearing.

God designed the unique rainforest plants to hold cures for many of the life-threatening diseases humans have contracted. What do you think is God's view about rainforest destruction?

Tree Projects

11.   In recent years there have been steps in the right direction, such as the Million Trees Project. Beginning in 2007, the Living Lands and Waters organization worked to plant its millionth tree by May 2016. Its mission included cleaning up waterways, removing invasive plants and planting native trees.[13]   Another project of hope is The Great Green Wall. This African-led initiative began in 2007 with the goal of restoring the natural landscape in one of the poorest areas of the continent.   Its success is measured in hectares (about 2 football fields of area): Ethiopia has 15 million hectares of restored land; Senegal has 25000 hectares of restored land, including 11.4 million trees; Nigeria has five million hectares of land restored; Sudan has 2000 hectares restored; and about 120 communities

of Burkina Faso, Mali and Niger are planting seeds and seedlings. Such a project with intentions to span several countries has been met with resistance in conflict-torn countries, and from hostile leaders. [14] [15]

Have you ever planted a tree? If so, do you still live near it, so that you could see its growth?

Fertilizers

12.   Looking at two passages in the Bible, it seems that God approves of fertilizers. Look at these to find the use of fertilizer:

> Luke 13:7-8 So he said to the man who took care of the vineyard, 'For three years now I have been coming back to look for this fig tree and haven't found any. Cut it down! Why should it use up the soil? ' 'Sir,' the man replied, 'leave it alone for one more year, and I will dig around it and fertilize it.'

> Jeremiah 8:2b The bones of these people will never be re-gathered and reburied. They will be like manure used to fertilize the ground.

So, even in Bible times man relied on natural fertilizer to aid crop growth. Animal waste, bones, fish parts and wood ash helped to replenish nutrients in the soil. In the early 1800s scientists determined three of the most beneficial nutrients: nitrogen, phosphorus, and potassium. By the mid 1900s chemical fertilizer production of these was in full swing, and agricultural productivity soared.

This result is good, however, the contamination of ground water with nitrates and phosphates is not good. The nitrogen from fertilizers, and even from manure, is converted by bacteria in the soil to nitrates. If there are more nitrates than the plants need, these will be washed away and flow into streams and rivers. Drinking water with excessive nitrates can be dangerous to humans. Pollution of drinking water by nitrates can also result from industrial waste, sewage disposal, detergents and manure.   Not only can nitrates enter drinking water, but they can cause algae growth. In slow moving lakes this algae can deprive fish of oxygen.

Phosphorus acts differently in that it attaches to the soil. When the soil erodes, the phosphorus moves with it, landing in streams, etc. While not dangerous, it will stimulate the growth of algae. Algae invasion can severely affect the water's environment, most obviously causing fishkill in warm weather when the oxygen level in the water is reduced.   [16]

In recent years sulfur additives are in use worldwide to increase agricultural production. However, this is kind of like finding a new way to achieve the effects of acid rain. Targeted applications on some crops have created dangerous effects. In the Florida Everglades, extensive applications on the sugarcane crops show up to ten times the acid rain sulfur levels. The sulfur leads to high production of methylmercury in the environment of marine wildlife. Fish and wildlife that eat fish, as well as human consumers of these fish, are seriously affected by the methylmercury. (See "Lesson 8:

God's Vision of the Earth: Fifth Day - Mercury in Fish") . There needs to be better monitoring in areas where sulfur use is prevalent, such as for corn in the midwest and for grapes in California. [17]

Where is the balance point for fertilizer use as respects more productive cropland versus environmental harm? Do you believe governments should be involved in such monitoring and regulation?

Algae Blooms

13.   Did you hear about the algae blooms in Florida in 2019? Have you seen these in person? If you have not, it does not really look like "blooms" floating, but simply like cloudy blue/green water. (Look at the photos in the link shown below.)   The blue-green cyanobacterial harmful algal bloom (cyanoHAB) can be harmful to humans, animals and fish through ingestion, inhalation or skin contact. Some of the effects are: nausea, vomiting, pneumonia, dermatitis, conjunctivitis, earache, sore throat, electrolyte imbalances, headache, and muscle weakness/ pain in joints and limbs. Is this enough to cause you to avoid the algae blooms?

Humans should avoid swimming, boating or doing water sports in areas where the smell and look of the water is foul. Also, avoid having dogs or other pets in contact with such water. Have you ever been near affected bodies of water?

Between 1984 and 2012 the intensity of algae blooms increased in ⅔ of inland freshwater lakes. Years of accumulation of fertilizer runoff, increased rainfall and warmer water temperatures all contribute to the problem. However, a study showed that when all other factors were nearly equal for different lakes, algae was much more prevalent in warmer waters. [18]   This finding supports policies and practices to limit further warming of our environment.   Have you ever lived or vacationed in an area with algae blooms?   How do you feel about this problem?   Would you consider making changes in your life which could help this?

Pesticides

14.   Have you heard of the notorious "Agent Orange?" For years the United States used this product for vegetation and brush clearing during the war in Vietnam. Ultimately the long-lasting harmful effects which had been covered up by Dow and Monsanto came to light. The list of cancers and other illnesses found to be directly linked to agent orange is exhaustive. [19]   I believe the use of this product by our government, which one would hope would have done sufficient testing and monitoring of the product, is unacceptable. Do you know anyone who had agent orange exposure? How do you feel about the US government's role in this fiasco?

Dow Round Up

15.   This pesticide product has been in the news for a few years. Unless you have been following the reports, you may not be aware of the concerns. Round-Up is a weed killer which inhibits an enzyme needed for plant growth. Its active ingredient, glyphosate, has been classified as a "probable human carcinogen" by the International Agency for Research on Cancer in 2015. Testing prior to its release only focused on the glyphosate, thus, leaving the effects of the product itself unknown.

After some years on the market numerous complaints came to light. It is now clear that glyphosate combined with the Round Up components causes irreversible damage to DNA cells in vitro, to the tune of 1000 times more toxic than the isolated ingredients. Effects can include: disruption of hormonal systems and beneficial gut bacteria, damage to DNA, developmental and reproductive toxicity, birth defects, cancer and neurotoxicity. The endocrine (hormonal) effects are most concerning since they appear with low exposure. Ecuadorian farmers exposed to aerial spraying developed severe poisoning reactions including vomiting, diarrhea, heart palpitations, numbness, blurred vision and fever. Perhaps good news: Bayer chemical company will be paying over $10 billion to settle tens of thousands of claims. However, the company still persists in selling the product, with no warning labels. [20]

The irony is that several weeds have become resistant to the original product. Never fear, Bayer and another competitor, Corteva, have developed other, more potent products. Bayer's product, XtendiMax, contains dicamba, found to be easily transferred to neighboring crops, prompting thousands of crop injury investigations. Corteva's product contains 2,4-D, a component in agent orange. So far the World Health Organization has declared Corteva's product to be, "Possibly carcinogenic to humans." Bayer's dicamba has not been evaluated.[21]   However, independent studies have found dicamba links to Non-Hodgkin's Lymphoma, hypothyroidism, lung cancer and colon cancer. [22]

How do you feel about Round Up use? Do you think it should be banned? Have you ever used this, or a product with dicamba, 2,4-D or glyphosate?

Do you think God sees man's use of such pesticides as good or as evil?

16.   The chemical compound chlorpyrifos has several common uses: to control indoor cockroaches, fleas and termites; to control agricultural pests, insects and worms; and to protect pets through flea and tick collars. Unfortunately it has been found to result in autoimmune disorders for people with frequent contact. In large amounts it could cause acute toxicity and neurological effects in fetuses, while only small amounts can cause these same effects in children. [23]   While most home

uses were banned in 2001, it is still used in the United States. For some reason it has become a political issue:

> On 29 March 2017, EPA Administrator Scott Pruitt denied a petition to ban chlorpyrifos.[1] However, on 9 August 2018, the U.S. 9th Circuit Court of Appeals ordered the EPA to ban the sale of chlorpyrifos in the United States within 60 days, though this ruling was almost immediately appealed by the Trump administration. [24]

And, in the European Union:
> On August 2, 2019, the European Food Safety Authority (EFSA) published a report concluding that no safe exposure level could be determined for chlorpyrifos...On December 6, 2019, the European Union (EU) announced that it will no longer permit sales of chlorpyrifos after January 31, 2020. [25]

Do you feel that chlorpyrifos should be banned in the United States? Do you feel that governments should regulate such products?

Conclude and Respond

At first glance humans may not recognize God's intention for their local forests. Yet, further study reveals the definite purpose for the vegetation in each area: the cloud forests, the boreal forests, the cedar forests, the rainforests, etc. Consider this week the value of the vegetation where you live. Take time to enjoy the beauty in it. If you are a gardener, ask God how to care for plants without all of the harmful chemicals.

Lesson 6 – Action Steps
- Buy only recycled or alternative (bamboo) paper products to save boreal forests which are commonly harvested for paper production.
- Write to lawmakers asking for a ban of the use of "Round-Up-type" glyphosate products on our food supply.
- Support tree planting projects, such as One Tree Planted.
- Write to lawmakers in support of developing countries' reduction of tree clearing as per agreements in the Glasgow Climate Conference (COP26).

[1] Shreya Dasgupta, "How Many Plant Species Are There in the World? Scientists Now Have an Answer, May 12, 2016, https://news.mongabay.com/2016/05/many-plants-world-scientists-may-now-answer/

[2] Tommy Trenchard, " 'There's No More Water': Climate Change on a Drying Island," New York Times, April 16, 2020, https://www.nytimes.com/2020/04/16/world/africa/comoros-climate-change-rivers.html)

[3] Anne Barnard, "Climate Change Is Killing the Cedars of Lebanon," July 18, 2018, https://www.nytimes.com/interactive/2018/07/18/climate/lebanon-climate-change-environment-cedars.html#:~:text=But%20some%20trees%20can%20survive,reserve%20has%20just%202%2C100%20trees.

⁴ Dion Nissenbaum and Nazih Osseiran, "A Row Over Trees Could Spark the Next Israel-Lebanon War," The Wall Street Journal, June 28, 2020, https://www.wsj.com/articles/a-row-over-trees-could-spark-the-next-israel-lebanon-war-11593345635)

⁵ Jennifer Skene, "THE ISSUE WITH TISSUE: HOW AMERICANS ARE FLUSHING FORESTS DOWN THE TOILET," February 2019, p. 8,   https://www.nrdc.org/sites/default/files/issue-tissue-how-americans-are-flushing-forests-down-toilet-report.pdf)

⁶ Skene, "The Issue With Tissue," page 11.

⁷ Michael Fleshman, "Saving Africa's Forests, the 'Lungs of the World,' " Africa Renewal Magazine, January 2008, https://www.un.org/africarenewal/magazine/january-2008/saving-africa%E2%80%99s-forests-%E2%80%98lungs-world%E2%80%99

⁸ Mouhamadou Kane, "The Silent Destruction of Senegal's Last Forests," January 10, 2019, https://enactafrica.org/enact-observer/the-silent-destruction-of-senegals-last-forests)

⁹ Fleshman, "Saving Africa's Forests."

¹⁰ The Visual and Data Journalism Team, "The Amazon in Brazil is on fire - how bad is it?" , BBC news https://www.bbc.com/news/world-latin-america-49433767

¹¹ "Top 10 Medicinal Plants of the Amazon," Prepared by RainforestsCruises.com, February 17, 2016, https://www.rainforestcruises.com/jungle-blog/top-10-medicinal-plants-of-the-amazon

¹² "Rosy Periwinkle," prepared by The Living Rain Forest, accessed May 2020, https://livingrainforest.org/learning-resources/rosy-periwinkle

¹³ "Million Trees Project," Prepared by Livinglandsandwaters.org, https://www.livinglandsandwaters.org/what-we-do/our-projects/milliontrees-project.html)

¹⁴ "The Great Green Wall Initiative," Prepared by United Nations Convention to Combat Desertification, accessed September 2020, https://www.unccd.int/actions/great-green-wall-initiative

¹⁵ "What Happened to Africa's Ambitious Green Belt Project?" , Prepared by Deutsche Welle, accessed August 2020, https://www.dw.com/en/what-happened-to-africas-ambitious-green-belt-project/a-53004690

¹⁶ "Environmental Problems with Fertilizers," Prepared by Argo Services International, accessed August 2020, https://www.agroservicesinternational.com/Environment/Problems.html#:~:text=Problems%20with%20fertilizers,water%20with%20nitrates%20and%20phosphates.&text=These%20algae%20eventually%20die%20and,This%20process%20is%20called%20eutrophication.

¹⁷ Daryl Lovell, "Agriculture Replaces Fossil Fuels as Largest Human Source of Sulfur to the Environment," University of Colorado Boulder, August 10, 2020, ttps://www.colorado.edu/today/2020/08/10/agriculture-replaces-fossil-fuels-largest-human-source-sulfur-environment

¹⁸ K. Wheeling, "Toxic Algal Blooms Are Worsening with Climate Change," November 13, 2019, https://eos.org/articles/toxic-algal-blooms-are-worsening-with-climate-change

¹⁹ "Agent Orange Exposure and VA Disability Compensation," Prepared by the Department of Veterans Affairs, September 18, 2020, https://www.va.gov/disability/eligibility/hazardous-materials-exposure/agent-orange/

²⁰ "Myth: Roundup is safe herbicide with low toxicity to animals and humans," GMO Myths and Truths, Prepared by Earthopensource.org, accessed September 2020, https://earthopensource.org/gmomythsandtruths/sample-page/4-health-hazards-roundup-glyphosate/4-1-myth-roundup-safe-herbicide-low-toxicity-animals-humans/#:~:text=Glyphosate%20and%20its%20main%20metabolite,and%20in%20mice%20in%20vivo.&text=Such%20damage%20to%20DNA%20may,of%20cancer%20and%20birth%20defects.

²¹ Jacob Bunge, "Roundup Ruled the Farm, Now Its Maker Has a Challenger," The Wall Street Journal, January 6, 2020, https://www.wsj.com/articles/roundup-ruled-the-farm-now-its-maker-has-a-challenger-11578328409#:~:text=Roundup%20revolutionized%20farming%20when%2C%20combined,It%20is%20still%20No.&text=Many%20in%20the%20industry%20expect,weeds%20than%20most%20other%20herbicides.

²² Carey Gillam, "Dicamba Fact Sheet," Prepared by US Right To Know, June 12, 2020, https://usrtk.org/pesticides/dicamba/

²³ National Library of Medicine, s.v. "Chlorpyrifos, Compound Summary", accessed June 2020, https://pubchem.ncbi.nlm.nih.gov/compound/Chlorpyrifos

²⁴ Wikipedia, s,v, "Chlorpyrifos," accessed June 2020, https://en.wikipedia.org/wiki/Chlorpyrifos

²⁵ Kelly Garson and Timothy Backstrom, "European Union to Ban Chlorpyrifos after January 31, 2020," January 6, 2020, https://www.jdsupra.com/legalnews/european-union-to-ban-chlorpyrifos-54320/

Lesson 7: God's Vision of the Earth: Fourth Day

I am fortunate. We live in a forested area where seasonal changes are painted in the oranges, yellows, reds and browns of autumn. Less publicized are the "baby" greens of the new spring leaves, called in my old Crayola 64-box, "spring green." So, I consider myself fortunate because many people do not get to see these marvels without traveling to deciduous forest areas. Since fall leaf excursions are a favorite social media post, all of us can "experience" these changes virtually through the internet.   Other friends' posts show little seasonal change, as I see snow-less Christmas scenes with palm trees in the background. Whatever type of seasonal changes you experience where you live, it is all part of God's plan.

1.   On the first day God separated light and darkness, calling the light 'Day" and the darkness "Night." He advanced this design on the fourth day to have the purposes of signs, seasons, days and years.   Read Genesis 1:14-19.

2.   These later passages further describe God's plan for our seasons. Read and make note of other signs of the seasons:
>   Genesis 8:22
>
>   Song of Solomon 2:11-13

3.   Psalmist David describes the sun from a man on earth's perspective in Psalm 19:6:
>   It rises at one end of the heavens and makes its circuit to the other;
>   nothing is deprived of its warmth.

For many years humans believed that God put us in the center of the universe. Then, in the third century BC scientists first proposed a model with the sun at the center and the earth orbiting around it. God set the earth in orbit around the sun. One full orbit accounts for one year. Besides designing the orbit, God also put the earth's axis on a tilt to give us seasons. Compare this design with the best of man's creations: the motor car, the airplane or the cell phone!

In case you do not remember from school days, you can picture this by using a ball as the sun and a broom as the earth's axis. With the ball in the center (perhaps on a table), hold the broom handle tilted away from the ball. In this position the top part of the broom, like the northern hemisphere, is farthest from the sun and would be in the colder winter months. The bottom portion of the broom, the southern hemisphere, is closest to the sun and would be in the warmer summer months. Now move to the opposite side of the ball, maintaining the same tilt of the broom. Everything is reversed: the top, the northern hemisphere, is closest to the sun for summer weather, whereas the bottom, the southern hemisphere, is farthest from the sun for winter weather.

Perhaps you marvel at this impressive design as I do. Depending where you live on the earth, seasons have quite different meanings. If you live near the Equator, the weather through all seasons is fairly consistent. If you live in a temperate zone, then weather changes from cold winter months to warm summer months. In areas near the poles, temperatures will also vary seasonally, with the north pole averaging warmer temperatures than the south simply due to land/water/currents/airflow differences.   Have you ever spent time either at the Equator or at the poles? If so, what was your impression of the weather?

4.　　This design surely had a purpose. Look for God's purpose in these verses:

Jeremiah 5:24

Acts 14:16-17

What could have been God's purpose in designing the Earth to have seasons? How would food production around the world be different if there was no change of seasons?

Some areas of the earth have little seasonal change. How would your life be different if average temperatures were the same year around?

5.　　Fortunately man has not been able to affect God's design for the sun, moon and seasons. However, with the blanket of greenhouse gases around the earth, the intensity of the seasons has changed. That is: average temperatures for all seasons are higher, and, thus, have affected man's activities. For example, the growing season for grapes in Europe has been impacted. Warmer temperatures impact European wine production: heat stress, less rainfall, more evapotranspiration, increased water requirements. Additionally, the regions which can support grapes for wine production are shifting north. [1] What will happen 10, 20 or 30 years from now if warmer temperatures affect growing seasons? Do you think farmers will be able to move their production to northern areas?

Allergies and Asthma

6.   Are you affected by seasonal allergies?   If so, have you noticed any change over the past ten years, such as a longer season or a stronger reaction? It is not your imagination. Scientists have found that pollen counts have been increasing over the past 20 years, predominantly from warmer temperatures and more carbon dioxide in the air. They have also studied the "pollen season." In 2000 the peak of annual pollen production which began on April 14 was May 1. With the current trend in these dates, by 2040 the peak in annual pollen production will be April 8.   In addition an analysis of seasons shows earlier spring weather and later start of winter weather. Do you think there is any way to explain this other than climate change? [2]

Warmer temperatures also impact production of fungal spores, mold spores and air pollution. Flooding and severe storms can increase the quantity and spread of triggers for asthma and allergies. Other greenhouse gases can prompt respiratory symptoms for people with lung diseases, causing reduced lung function or death.[3]

What could you do to help reduce the increase of allergies and asthma?

Daylight

7.   God created a daily cycle of light and darkness by having the earth spin on its axis. This action exposes one position on the globe to sunlight for some part of the day, while it leaves that same position in darkness for the remainder of the day. Think of people living in the far north, such as in Alaska or Greenland. In Fairbanks, Alaska, in December the earth's axis is tilting away from the sun so that on December 21 there are less than 4 hours of daylight. In contrast in June when the earth is on the opposite side of the sun with the top of the axis tilting toward the sun, there are more than 21 hours of daylight. Have you ever lived or visited an area near one of the poles having this variety of daylight hours? If so, was it difficult to adjust?

Moon

8.   Genesis 1:16 refers to a "lesser light to rule the night." Other than serving as a "lesser light" in our sky, the moon has another role. The gravitational pull of the moon causes tides: high tides occur when the moon is exactly on our side of the earth, and also when the moon is directly on the opposite side of the earth. Since the moon completes one orbit in a little less than one day, there are two times of high tide each day. What do you think was God's purpose in creating the moon?

Years ago, in response to our daughter's class study of Nova Scotia, we traveled there for our vacation. What we discovered in the fishing port of Digby was another aspect of God's brilliant design:

bay tides. The Bay of Fundy has the highest tide in the world at above 50 feet. Locals there contrived a floating dock attached to huge vertical pilings. The dock rises or falls with the tide, all the while holding fast to the boats tied there. If we walked by at 9 am (high tide), then later at 3 pm (low tide) we saw a dramatically different site in relation to nearby buildings. In the same manner, we walked on a nearby sandy beach in the afternoon which became a lake at sunset. It is hard for me, a human being, to conceive of all of the intricacies of God's creation.

Have you ever seen the Bay of Fundy? Have you seen other tidal areas and noted the differences from high tide to low tide?   Can you imagine God's plan for tides?

Note: The remainder of this lesson focuses on power sources that use or are modeled after the sun. All other power sources are covered in Lessons 13 and 14.

Nuclear Power

9.   My town is in the process of shutting down its nuclear power plant, which had been in operation for the twenty years we have lived here. We were given potassium iodide pills to take in the event of a nuclear accident here. While these are an antidote against thyroid cancer due to exposure to radioactive iodine, they do not protect against all discharge.   Would you move to an area with a nuclear power plant?

10.   Read these bible verses to determine and make note of God's design for the sun:

Genesis 1:16

Genesis 31:40

Nuclear Fusion

11.   God designed the sun to produce heat energy through a process called **nuclear fusion**. It is easy to picture the process: hydrogen atoms are "fused" together into larger atoms, generating heat energy. Mimicking God's fusion design, scientists now believe after 60 years of research they can copy God's design for heat production in the sun. On July 28, 2020 the ITER Project in southern France began assembling prepared components for this giant fusion reactor. This reactor will use the elements lithium and deuterium (heavy hydrogen), and yield only energy and the inert gas helium. [4]

The goal is to show that a fusion reactor can generate more power than the amount of electricity needed to operate it, and, thus, make it a viable clean energy source. No other fusion projects on earth have yet produced a viable amount of energy. We will not know whether it works until 2025, after the five year assembly process. If feasible, we would have an energy source which does not emit carbon, has no meltdown potential, and produces much less radioactive waste. [5]

So, man may have achieved the same process for energy production that God designed for the sun. What do you think about that?

Nuclear Fission

12. You may be wondering about nuclear power plants which exist today. Those in use today employ a different method, nuclear fission, to produce power. The process splits an easily "breakable" type of uranium atom, U 235, to release energy. The nucleus of the atom is split into two pieces. Although this process generates energy, it results in radioactive waste, the storage of which is perhaps the greatest concern for nuclear power. Various technologies are used, some that even include recycling. Despite the potential for leakage, nuclear is safer than most other power sources, especially when air pollution is considered. [6]

How do you feel about the use of nuclear power in our world?

Solar Energy

13. The nuclear fusion energy production presented above follows the **process** God uses in the sun. In contrast, the **harnessing** of the sun's energy as it enters the earth's atmosphere generates solar energy. Perhaps God is happy that man has been able to use the sun he created in two ways! In line with all of God's intricate design for the earth, He engineered the sun to provide us with sunlight. Read Isaiah 30:26 (NIV):

> The moon will shine like the sun, and the sunlight will be seven times brighter, like the light of seven full days, when the Lord binds up the bruises of his people and heals the wounds he inflicted.

Why did God include this bright light for our days?   What purposes do you know for sunlight?

Did you ever try the trick of using a magnifying glass to ignite a fire? If you did, then you witnessed the power of sunlight. Again, this is one of God's astonishing creations.

14. As is usually the case with inventions, beginning in the late 1800s several scientists built upon each other's efforts to create photoelectric cells which could turn light from the sun into electric power. Creating these cells from silicon by Bell Labs in the 1950s helped make practical use a reality. With the "space race" in the 1950s and 1960s, powering spacecraft with solar cells became feasible. In

fact, in 1964 NASA powered the Nimbus satellite entirely with photovoltaic solar cells. [7] Continuing improvements since then have made solar electricity a viable energy source. [8]

Do you have solar panels? Why would you be in favor of using these? What could stop you from installing these on your house?

15. Did you ever use a solar calculator or solar watch? Recall that it needed to be in good light in order to operate. However, do you remember that it did not need to be sunlight? Small devices can use artificial sources of light which mimic the wavelengths of sunlight. In these solar-powered devices, man once again copied God's design. [9]

Unfortunately, the solar industry has been affected by political pressure. Did you know that President Carter installed solar panels on the White House in 1979 for heating water used in the kitchen, the laundry and the first family's quarters? President Reagan removed these in 1986, which was explained at the time as being necessary for repairs, although the administration was adverse to renewable energy advances. Fortunately in 2002 President Bush installed solar water heaters for the pool, and, then, in 2014 President Obama installed more powerful solar photovoltaic panels on the roof. [10] The 2018 tariffs imposed on Chinese solar panels by President Trump's administration raised the cost of solar installation enough to cause the loss of the 60000 installer jobs. [11]

Are you getting the feeling that politics certainly affect environmental policies?   In light of high initial cost for solar panel installation, how do you feel about the government installing them on government buildings?

16. I am pleased to acknowledge that my church installed solar panels six years ago. Also, the school boards in my town and the neighboring town elected to install solar panels a few years ago. Do you think adding solar panels would be a wise investment for your church?   Should your local school system install solar panels?

Conclude and Respond

For a human being to conceive the earth's design for days, nights and seasons would be impossible. That is why it took man much study over many years to detail God's work. Man's study in more recent power-hungry years has enabled him to tap into the sun's power. Perhaps solar power and nuclear fusion would be looked on as "good energy" in God's eyes. Spend some time this week in the sunlight. Soak in the seasonal changes for whatever time of year it is. If you live near a tidal body of water, visit there at high and low tides to see God's role for the moon. Thank God for his gift of the seasons, the sun and the moon. Pray about actions you could take to influence governmental policy on energy sources.

Lesson 7 – Action Steps

- Slow the expansion of allergy season through actions to stop global warming such as using manual- powered tools, driving electric, installing solar panels, eating less beef, etc.
- Write to lawmakers about SAFE use of nuclear power.
- Request that lawmakers install solar panels on government buildings.

[1] "Viniculture: European Scale," Prepared by Climate Change Post, Center for Climate Adaptation, https://www.climatechangepost.com/europe/viniculture/

[2] Aaron Bernstein MD, "Climate Change and Allergies," Harvard TH Chan School of Public Health, https://www.hsph.harvard.edu/c-change/subtopics/climate-change-and-allergies/

[3] "Does Climate Change Impact Allergic Disease?" Prepared by American Academy of Allergy Asthma and Immunology, https://www.aaaai.org/conditions-and-treatments/library/allergy-library/climate-change

[4] Florian Ion Petrescu, "Nuclear Fusion," Bucharest Polytechnic University, July 31, 2012, https://www.altenergymag.com/article/2012/07/nuclear-fusion/1090#:~:text=Raw%20materials%20for%20fusion%20are,far%20superior%20to%20nuclear%20fission.

[5] Damain Carrington, "World's Largest Nuclear Fusion Project Begins Assembly in France," The Guardian, July, 28, 2020, https://www.theguardian.com/environment/2020/jul/28/worlds-largest-nuclear-fusion-project-under-assembly-in-france

[6] Wikipedia, s.v. "Nuclear Energy, Environmental Impact," accessed June 2020, https://en.wikipedia.org/wiki/Nuclear_power#Environmental_impact

[7] "History of Solar Energy: Who Invented Solar Panels?," Prepared by Vinint.Solar, accessed July 2020, https://www.vivintsolar.com/learning-center/history-of-solar-energy

[8] Elizabeth Chu and D. Lawrence Tarazano, "A Brief History of Solar Panels," Smithsonian Magazine, April 22, 2019, https://www.smithsonianmag.com/sponsored/brief-history-solar-panels-180972006/

[9] John Papiewski, "What Kind of Light Does a Solar Cell Need?," March 10, 2018, https://sciencing.com/kind-light-solar-cell-need-21539.html

[10] Derick Lila, "THE SAGA OF THE WHITE HOUSE SOLAR PANELS—A SOLAR STORY," June 5, 2017, https://pvbuzz.com/the-saga-of-the-white-house-solar-panels/#:~:text=The%20White%20House%20itself%20harvests,on%20the%20White%20House%20roof.&text=The%20White%20House%20did%20not%20have%20solar%20panels%20in%202000.

[11] Miranda Green, "Analysis: Trump solar tariffs cost 62K US jobs," The Hill, December 3, 2019, https://thehill.com/policy/energy-environment/472691-analysis-trump-solar-tariffs-cost-62k-us-jobs

Lesson 8: God's Vision of the Earth: Fifth Day

Have you ever been snorkeling? Even though I do regular lap swimming, when the opportunity for snorkeling presented itself, I was apprehensive. I watched others paddle around with their breathing tubes rising above water level. I imagined it would be quite difficult to keep the tube above water level, and thus not "breathing in" water. Entranced with that prospect, the voice of our instructor broke through, "Put your face in the water, then, paddle out to see the treasures below!"

Even though there are certainly "treasures" to see **above** ground, I found that the ocean floor presented a spectacular view. God created such a wide array of ocean life, between the forever-in-motion fish of all sizes and colors, to the frilly filigree coral. The motion picture represented a thriving environment, which I had never previously considered. Most importantly I realized that God was the mastermind behind this complex salt-water habitat. To see where this habitat fits in creation, we return to Genesis.

1. The creation story continues with God's masterpiece on the fifth day. Read Genesis 1:20-23.

Read these two selections, then answer these questions: What do the fish of the sea tell us? What do the birds of the air teach us? Do you see God as in control of the fish and the birds?

Job 12:7-10.

Ecclesiastes 9:12

Do you believe man has impacted fish and birds?   If, so what does God think of the situation?

2. God did not just create a few kinds of fish, but He "let the waters swarm." The image that comes to mind is looking into a tank at an aquarium. Have you ever visited an aquarium?

My image shows **numerous** fish zigzagging around each other in a scene of endless movement (Do fish ever sleep?). Not only did God put such a variety of fish in the waters, He created the nearly invisible microbes that keep the balance of nature in the earth's waters.   Describe what you know of God's plan for the balance of nature in our waters. Think about sources of nutrients, food chain, relationships of different creatures and how they multiply.

Coral

3.   What was God's design for coral? Many people believe that coral is a plant. However, coral is actually an animal which survives through a symbiotic relationship with algae. This means that they support each other. Coral begins as the animal, polyp. Polyps attach to a hard surface like a rock, then excrete protective calcium skeletons. The variety of polyps create a variety of skeletons which appear as the bleached white coral we know.

Wait, you say! Coral is not "bleached white!" No, this is part of the symbiotic relationship.   The algae, called zooxanthella, live inside of the skeleton, thriving through the photosynthesis of sunlight and carbon dioxide from the coral (or polyps). Their presence gives the skeletons their color. Additionally, they give the coral oxygen, amino acids and glucose, the by-products of photosynthesis.

In recent years much of the coral in the oceans has lost its color. God's balance for the coral and the algae has been disturbed. Warming of the water by 1 - 2 degrees makes the algae (zooxanthella) toxic to the coral, The coral then expels the algae, leaving it bleached white. If these conditions persist, the coral will be starved and die.   Other destructive forces are: storms/powerful waves, imbalance of predator fish populations and pollution from land runoff.[1]

God has also designed coral to be a food/protection source for other marine life:

> Coral reefs support more species per unit area than any other marine environment, including about 4,000 species of fish, 800 species of hard corals and hundreds of other species. [2]

Compared to God's original design, what do coral reefs look like now? What would God say about the loss of coral?

Do you value the beauty of coral? What would you do if you knew that chemicals you use on your lawn and garden eventually enter the oceans and harm coral?

Coral loss results from warmer ocean waters. Warmer ocean waters result from carbon emissions from cars and power plants that add to global warming . Does coral loss prompt you to make any changes in your life to reduce carbon emissions?

Warming of Fish Habitat

4.   The ocean water becomes warmer because 90% of the excess heat in the atmosphere is absorbed by the oceans. So, as the atmosphere warms, so does the ocean. Let's look at statistics about warming ocean water.   Record worldwide sea temperatures were recorded in 2016, at 1.55 degrees F above average. This is closely followed by that recorded in March of 2020: 1.49 degrees F. above the average. Warmer ocean waters are more acidic, contain less oxygen and reduce marine life diversity, cause sea level rise, flooding, ocean circulation changes (Gulf Stream) changes weather patterns. [3]

Here are some impacts of warming waters:

- Kelp forests in the coastal waters of California and Oregon have vanished, replaced by sea urchins who ate everything.
- Cod fisheries in Alaska and Shrimp fisheries in Maine have seen their catch greatly reduced in warmer waters.
- Tasmanian kelp forests which covered 9 million sq. meters have been reduced to 500,000 sq. meters.
- Hot water flow off of the Uruguayan coast killed clams and mussels.
- The number of large fish in the ocean has decreased by 90% since 1950 (concurrently impacted by overfishing).
- Grey whales in the Pacific Ocean experienced an unprecedented mortality rate five times the normal rate in 2019. This was attributed to Arctic ice melt, which released a nutrient that triggered algae bloom. The algae bloom triggered krill movement north to feed on it. The whales feed on the krill, and, thus, were left in more northern, colder waters at the end of their migration. [4]

Do any of these listed impacts concern you? What does God think of these changes to His design?

Acidity

5.   Another aspect of the warming waters is acidification: ocean waters are 25% more acidic on average than before the Industrial Revolution.   As the water absorbs carbon dioxide from the air, a chemical process leaves more hydrogen ions floating in the ocean. More of these means that the pH of the water becomes more acidic.   The basic problem is that acid decays calcium skeletons. One critically affected sea creature is the pteropod. Never heard of them? Many larger sea creatures, from krill to whales, depend on pteropods as the base of their diet. Acidity is slowly dissolving their shells, leaving them vulnerable. [5]

Are you familiar with the Disney fish, Nemo? Nemo is perhaps the most famous clown fish, albeit fictional! Unfortunately, acidity impacts clown fish. High acidity affects their instinct, leading them to stray far from home because they cannot discriminate the smell of kin. Their instinct is also affected so that they do not distinguish predators as easily. [6] Many children would be unhappy to know that acidity from warming oceans, from global warming, is killing these fish.

What could you tell a child can be done to help this? Is there anything we could do to stop oceans from warming?

Mercury Levels in Fish

6.   Mercury that naturally occurs in the earth's crust is released into the air through mining and the burning of fossil fuels. [7] From the air it seeps into land and water. Bacteria in the water change it to methylmercury. Logically, fish that have been alive longer, and fish that eat other fish have higher levels of methylmercury. This chemical is toxic to the central nervous system, and can cause permanent damage to the brain and spinal cord. It is especially harmful to unborn babies and infants, so pregnant and nursing moms should be careful.   Everyone should monitor their fish consumption based on mercury levels shown in noted article: "The Best Types of Fish to Avoid Mercury," by Mark Stibich, PhD. [8]

Do you eat seafood? How would you feel if seafood was no longer available?   Do you monitor mercury levels in the fish you eat?

7.   After God has flooded the earth, leaving only Noah's family with pairs of all creatures to populate it, God speaks to Noah. Read Genesis 9:2-3.

This passage uses the phrases, "the fear of you," and "the dread of you," to describe how all creatures will look at man. Ecclesiastes 9:12 takes this idea a step further:

> Moreover, no one knows when their hour will come: As fish are caught in a cruel net, or birds are taken in a snare, so people are trapped by evil times that fall unexpectedly upon them.

Based upon these passages, what seems to be God's design for fish?

Birds

8.   Have you ever watched a bird build a nest? Have you seen the nest filled with eggs? Have you witnessed a mother feeding her young? Have you viewed a flock of birds migrating to a different climate? One of my favorite sites is a great white egret framed by golden sea grasses above the blue bay water. The regal bird nonchalantly poses while many cameras click to memorialize the image. Perhaps you are not near seawater, but have been privileged to see a pink flamingo balance or an

eagle hover. Beauty is only one aspect of God's design. These birds fill other critical purposes in our lives: pollinating plants, distributing seeds, controlling pests and filling a position in the food chain.

Genesis 1:20 states that God created the birds to "fly above the earth across the expanse of the heavens." . Read these verses and find more about God's purpose for birds:

Psalm 104:12

Leviticus 1:14

James 3:7

Of these purposes, which still apply now in the 21st century?

9.   These verses give us God's direction about birds. Read each and decide what is His direction:

Deuteronomy 22:6

Leviticus 11:13-19

Matthew 6:26

Matthew 10:29

What image do these verses give of God caring for birds? What could you draw from this image about man's care for birds?

10. This is a common site: a birdhouse mounted next to the garden. Do you have one by your garden? I do. But, did you know the purpose for this? Birds are a natural control for insects. In fact a study showed that birds eat 400-500 million TONS of insects per year. [9] How many have they eaten from your garden without you knowing it?

One particularly troublesome bug, the spruce budworm, has been destroying spruce and fir trees in Canada, the US and Eurasia. Various pesticides used for control of the budworm have been related to harmful effects on local fish, mammal and people populations. However, several bird species, the evening grosbeak and the warbler, have helped control these in years of less extensive outbreaks. [10] What is your opinion about using pesticides to control nasty pests? Do you think it is wiser to encourage these natural predator birds?

11.   It is very obvious that bees like the flowers and flowering plants around a garden, but did you know that birds also help with pollination? Birds favor sight over smell, so this helps with some flowers which do not attract bees because of their minimal scent. In fact about 5% of plants that we use for medicine or food are pollinated by birds. Besides flowers, birds pollinate the tropical crops of bananas, papayas and nutmeg. [11]   So, God's design enables birds to help with pollination. Have you ever seen a hummingbird in action?

12.   Have you ever seen a vulture or turkey buzzard devouring a roadside carcass? So, here is another benefit of birds. It may not seem that this is a frequent occurrence if you live in a city or the suburbs. However, in more rural areas this "free" clean up service is very valuable.

13.   I have found random flowers and tree seedlings growing in my yard, knowing for certain that I did not plant these. Do you ever find such random plants in your yard?   It is possible that seeds were carried by the wind, but it is also possible that birds are responsible. Birds eat seeds, then "plant" these in their droppings. In fact, the Micronesian Imperial-pigeon is responsible for many plants growing on this island chain, while birds are responsible for at least 70% of the growth in New Zealand forests.

Here is one story of an ecosystem in balance: In the salt marshes of the southeastern US an abundance of cordgrass filters local water and protects from sea erosion.   Periwinkle snails left unchecked could eliminate cordgrass, their favorite food, turning the marshes into mudflats. However, the local birds keep the area in balance with their snail diet. [12]

As I write this outdoors on my deck I am reminded of one more benefit of birds. Thank God for songbirds which try to drown out the local power tool noisemakers. I wonder what the birds think of all this loud noise. Have you experienced quiet moments when the bird melodies reach you? Have you done any amateur bird watching, even just from your window, or on a walk?

14.   How does the bird population now compare to how God designed it for Adam and Eve? Even though we do not have data for back then, there are 2.9 billion fewer birds, a drop of 29%, in the United States and Canada since 1970. This data comes from a Journal of Science study which compiled numerous bird count studies, including some made using weather radar. Sadly the loss has impacted even the seemingly abundant species like robins and sparrows. The factors which have had the greatest impact are habitat loss and pesticides.

Have you seen lands cleared for new development where most trees and brush are removed? The birds return from their travels and say, "Where is our house (nest)?" Relocation is not always possible, since new areas may mean more natural predators, or insufficient food supply. It would help if local ordinances could restrict tree removal (as noted in the example about my neighboring town in "Lesson 5 - God's Vision of the Earth on the Third Day: Vegetation (Part 1)- Local Tree Clearing"). Can you picture areas from your earliest memories where the landscape has changed? Most likely this has not been for the better. What could be done to stop this?

15. Bird populations have also suffered from pesticides. One of the worst culprits is neonicotinoid which is believed to affect weight gain for birds, and, thus, inhibits migration. One type of the neonicotinoids, imidacloprid, was found to be highly toxic to four bird species: Japanese quail, house sparrow, canary, and pigeon. [13]   Although the EPA banned 12 products containing neonicotinoid in 2019, 47 products are still available. [14]   How do you feel about the loss of bird populations?   If you are concerned, do you think it would be possible to influence government action about pesticides?

16.   Apparently there were environmentalists in 1918! At that time due to the near extinction of some bird species, the Migratory Bird Treaty Act was passed.   Prompted by pressure from the oil lobby, President Trump's administration, through the US Fish and Wildlife Service, attempted to exclude the "incidental" destruction of birds (June 2020). For example, a company which INCIDENTALLY kills thousands of birds in an oil spill would not be liable.[15]   Fortunately, President Biden's administration overruled the previous administration's proposed rule change. Do you believe such policies are affected by politics? Do you believe a citizen has a chance of influencing such policies?

Conclude and Respond

God created water teeming with marine life and skies criss-crossed with flying birds. However, the earth's warming waters are having trouble supporting that "teeming" marine population, which happens to be part of the world food supply.   Plus, the decline in bird population reduces seed transfer and weakens the food chain. God's creatures have always fit precisely in His food chain web. Do a bit of bird watching this week. Study their habits as they feed their young, build their nests, or migrate in flocks. Also, look for images of "coral" online. Enjoy the beautiful images. Then, thank God for the sea creatures and for the birds. Pray about what you can do to help the coral, or the fish, or the birds.

Lesson 8 – Action Steps
- Attract local birds with birdhouses and birdfeeders.
- Hang warning bell on cat and limit outside time.

- Limit use of fossil fuels for reduced release of mercury in the air, which ultimately would be found in fish. (Drive less or use electric, use manual-powered tools, and use renewable power at home.)
- Request limits for pesticides (neonicotnoid–type) from lawmakers.

[1] "Anthropogenic (Human) Threats to Corals," Prepared by National Ocean Service, accessed May 2020, https://oceanservice.noaa.gov/education/tutorial_corals/coral09_humanthreats.html

[2] "The Importance of Coral Reefs," Prepared by National Ocean Service, accessed June 2020, https://oceanservice.noaa.gov/education/tutorial_corals/coral07_importance.html

[3] Brian Sullivan, "World's Oceans Now Warmest on Record, Increasing Risk of Hurricanes, Wildfires," _Time,_ April 20, 2020, https://time.com/5824299/ocean-temperature-rise-climate-change/

[4] Andrea Marks and Hannah Murphy, "On the Eve of Extinction," _Rolling Stone_, April 2020, Issue 1338, p. 80.

[5] "Ocean Acidification," Prepared by National Oceanic and Atmospheric Administration, April 2020, https://www.noaa.gov/education/resource-collections/ocean-coasts/ocean-acidification#:~:text=Because%20of%20human%2Ddriven%20increased,the%20ocean%20becomes%20more%20acidic.)

[6] Jeffrey Goodell, "Rising Tides,Troubled Waters," by April 2020, _Rolling Stone_, p. 67.

[7] "Mercury Emissions: The Global Context," Prepared by the US Environmental Protection Agency, January 28, 2020, https://www.epa.gov/international-cooperation/mercury-emissions-global-context#:~:text=Mercury%20occurs%20naturally%20in%20the,can%20be%20washed%20into%20water.)

[8] Mark Stibich, PhD, "The Best Types of Fish to Avoid Mercury," _Very Well Fit_, April 13, 2020, https://www.verywellfit.com/the-best-types-of-fish-for-health-2223830.

[9] Jessica Law, "Why We Need Birds (Far More Than They Need Us)," January 4, 2019, https://www.birdlife.org/worldwide/news/why-we-need-birds-far-more-they-need-us)

[10] Wikipedia, s.v. "Spruce Budworm," accessed June 2020, https://en.wikipedia.org/wiki/Spruce_budworm

[11] Erica Cirino, "What Do the Birds and the Bees Have to Do With Global Food Supply?," Audubon.org, March 10, 2016, https://www.audubon.org/news/what-do-birds-and-bees-have-do-global-food-supply

[12] Law, "Why We Need Birds."

[13] Wikipedia, s.v. "Imidacloprid," accessed May 2019, https://en.wikipedia.org/wiki/Imidacloprid#Bees_and_other_insects

[14] Aria Bendix, "The US Just Banned 12 Pesticides that are Like Nicotine for Bees. Here's How Dangerous They Are," _Business Insider_, May 30, 2019, https://www.businessinsider.com/epa-banned-pesticides-killing-bees-2019-5#:~:text=The%20US%20Environmental%20Protection%20Agency,to%20the%20world's%20crop%20production

[15] Latham and Watkins, "US Fish and Wildlife Service Continues Work to Narrow Application of Migratory Bird Treaty Act," _Washington Post_, June 23, 2020, https://www.washingtonpost.com/news/energy-environment/wp/2018/04/13/the-trump-administration-officially-clipped-the-wings-of-the-migratory-bird-treaty-act/

Lesson 9 - God's Vision of the Earth on the Sixth Day: Animals

Cats are independent. That is our excuse for our cat, Tilly, living her sixth (seventh?) life right now. In her first life she disappeared when we pulled out the driveway to drive the two miles to the Girl Scout leader's house. Hours later we saw her double (which turned out to be really her) exploring the leader's yard, apparently having hitched a ride there in the secret crevasses of our car's undercarriage. The next time she tried a longer disappearance: two days and nights. All of our hunting around the neighborhood was to no avail. The next morning I heard loud meows, which I finally tracked to the highest tree in the neighbor's backyard. With no help from the fire truck, I lured her down with an open can of cat food, moving from side-to-side in the pattern of the branches. A bit unnerved by that experience, she chose a shorter tree in our backyard for a day and night to test her next life. The same technique brought her down, eager to eat and begin another life. Her next two were multiple day excursions to our two separate attics. After "helping" us with moving boxes up and down she found perfect places for naps while the doors were unknowingly closed. Loud meowing a day or so later ultimately pointed us to her new nap sites. Despite her runaway tendency, we love her, as I am sure you love your house pets!

> For every kind of beast and bird, of reptile and sea creature, can be tamed and has been tamed by mankind.   James 3:7 (ESV)

What would we do without our pets? God placed many types of animals on the earth, but certainly included varieties which man could tame to keep us company.

1. God's to-do-list for the sixth day was quite long! On the sixth day he created all animals which live and move on land, plus male and female humans. In addition, He gave humans direction about their responsibility. Read Genesis 1:24-31.

The verses note that God brings forth livestock, creatures that move along the ground and wild animals, each according to its kind. "According to its kind" likely refers to "its species." Besides your house pets, what is your favorite animal?

2. Isaiah 11:6-9 depicts a scene where animals and man live in harmony, a peaceful coexistence. Read this passage, then, note a few of the animal or animal/man pairs.

What is meant by the last verse (Isaiah 11:9): "They shall not hurt or destroy in all my holy mountain; for the earth shall be full of the knowledge of the Lord as the waters cover the sea?" How would you rate man's adherence to this direction?

Extinction

3.   Man became selfish with the poor passenger pigeon. In skies over the United States billions of these birds could be seen migrating between the gulf states and the Great Lakes region every year….until the early 1800s, that is. Americans figured out how to easily shoot or trap these for a ready food source, with little thought of Isaiah 11:9. The last passenger pigeon died in Cincinnati Zoological Garden in 1914.[1] What do you think could have been done to avoid its extinction?

Fortunately, the extinction of these obviously abundant bird species helped to promote the passage of the Migratory Bird Treaty Act of 1918.

4.   Can you name an animal which is extinct? Did you think of dinosaurs? Exactly where dinosaurs fit into the Bible writings is not clear. Anthropologists have found bones of many dinosaur species, so they have existed. These were likely part of God's creation of animals on the sixth day. Scientists believe they disappeared through a natural extinction, that is through a catastrophe event. Some species die out through what is called, "natural selection," a process that favors the strongest, most adaptable species. Lastly there is "human-caused extinction," through habitat destruction, pollution, pesticides, sea level rise and global warming.

These are some of the species named extinct in 2019:

> Hawaiian tree snail, Brazilian bird: alagoas foliage cleaner , Bramble Cay Melomys, Catarina pupfish (Mexican freshwater fish), chinese paddlefish (one of largest freshwater fish)- Yangtze river), Corquin robber frog, cryptic treehunter - brazilian bird, cunning silverside - Mexican freshwater fish, Indochinese tiger (extirpation), Lake Oku puddle frog, Miss Waldron's red colobus monkey, Poo-uli (Hawaiian bird), Summatran rhinoceros (extirpation- local extinction), Victorian grasslands earless dragon (Australia's first known reptile extinction), Villa Lopez pupfish, Yangtze giant softshell turtle [2]

Scientists report that at least 15,000 species are on the way to extinction today. Many researchers agree that this represents a rate that is hundreds of times greater than the long-term average. [3] Some people believe that humans are somewhat responsible for this fast pace: habitat destruction, pollution and pesticides. Plus, they believe that humans contribute to global warming and the resulting sea level rise, both of which can impact species. The opposite view is: "We do not need to do anything, since this is a natural process." Where do you stand on this? Do you feel strongly enough to take action on any endangered species?

Bacon Lovers' Quandary

5.   Do you eat pork, that is, bacon, ham, pulled pork, sausage? If so, do you know where the pork comes from? Most pork consumed in the United States is produced in Iowa, Minnesota and North

Carolina. [4] This production generates an abundance of pig waste, which is collected in lagoons on the farms.

So, what happens if that area is flooded? It's not a pretty site. This was the case in North Carolina after Hurricane Florence in 2018 and after Hurricane Floyd in 1999. Lagoon water entering rivers can cause mass fish die-offs, harmful algae bloom and pig drownings in the contaminated water. In addition, there is potential for contamination of water supplies. Florence flood waters also breached a coal ash pond causing the toxic waste from coal burning operations to leak into rivers. [5]

Do you remember hearing about the extensive flooding in the Midwest in 2020? Yes, it flooded in the bacon-producing Iowa. Yes, lagoons of pig waste overflowed there, too. [6]   What could be done to avoid the leaking of pig waste? Or, a bigger question: what should farmers do with the waste? Do you believe Americans will continue to eat bacon and pulled pork?

Have you ever been in a similar flood? If so, were you able to use your water supply? Do you think floods from hurricanes or other intense storms will continue to happen in the future?

Insects

6.	My daughter and I are insect magnets. That is, bugs love us and we never emerge from an evening outdoors without a few bites. Are you an insect magnet, or one of the fortunate ones like my husband who gets few bites?

7.	In Psalm 50:11 God tells us:
	I know every bird in the mountains, and the insects in the fields are mine. (NIV)

What image does that give you about the birds and insects?

Read and note the pertinence to insects in each of the following verses:

	Leviticus 11:20-23

	Job 25:5-6

	Matthew 3:4

	1 Samuel 12:14

	2 Chronicles 7:13-14

	Deuteronomy 7:20

If we try to discern God's purpose for insects from these verses, it seems that they are a tool for God's retribution, but could also be man's food. If we look at the scientific picture of insects' purpose, we find much value: seed-spreading, pollination and balancing the food chain for other insects, birds, reptiles, fish and mammals. No wonder that God's creation includes 900,000 different species of insects! [7]

Think for a minute about how many insect bites you have had recently, especially if you are a gardener or walk in the evenings. Also, think about how often you have had to clean bugs off of the windshield. Plus consider how many invasive flies you have swatted. From my perspective, I have been less bothered in the last ten years. Do you notice any difference?

Disappearing Insects

8.   Even though we may be "plagued" by insect bites, pesky indoor flies and windshield splatter, those 900,000 insect species God designed are important to our food chain. Unfortunately, numerous insect studies in the past decades have documented fewer insects. Data from 166 long-term surveys from over 1600 sites reveals that insects like butterflies, ants and grasshoppers are going down by 0.92% per year, which amounts to 9% per decade. At that pace, since I was a child, the insect population has declined by over 40%! [8] I guess I am not imagining it.

The picture is complex, with the losses varying by area. For example, losses are greater and affect more species by clear cutting tropical forests. Even though land-based insects are declining, freshwater insects are increasing, likely because of pollution controls. Freshwater insects only account for 10% or less of the total, so the decline dominates.

What do you think causes the losses? Yes, these land management practices hurt insect populations: urbanization, rainforest destruction, not-sustainable forestry. Wildfires can render an area empty of insects. Also, pesticides do exactly what their name implies, they kill pests both through direct application, and through water and soil transmission. Each dead insect means the lizard, bird or other insect has less to eat and may ultimately be affected, too. [9]

Spotted Lanternfly

9.   Recently while sitting on my daughter's balcony in Pennsylvania I commented on the "pretty bugs" sharing my bench. These pretty bugs are Spotted Lanternflies, an invasive species from China and Vietnam that is claiming territory in PA. "Invasive" means that they harm trees and vines, like apples and grapes, plus deposit "honeydew" which turns into mold on plants. If left unchecked, these pests could diminish much of the agricultural output of the area. I give this example to show that insect invasive species can truly affect our global food supply. [10]   It is a curious site when my

daughter and I are walking in the area to see many other walkers stamping the sidewalk in hopes that the residents can win out! Do have any other similar pests in your area?

Locusts

10. As I write this, Africa has experienced an historic locust plague which began in 2019. God knew what he was doing when he sent locust plagues on the misbehaving people of the Old Testament : Locust swarms can include up to one million bugs. The pests move over the land in huge swarms that appear like clouds, then dive to hover around animals and people. Looking at their picture in the referenced article, I would be terrified! Swarms of these plant eaters can devour as much food daily as 35000 people. Aerial control operations spray pesticides on the affected areas, which presents another concern about pesticides contaminating air, land and water. [11]

How did God want the insect population to function? Why do you think there are invasive species like the spotted lantern fly, the locust and the "murder hornet" (mentioned in the subsequent "Bees" section)? What do you think is the long-term picture for insects on the Earth?

Bees

11. Maybe you, like me, remember all of the bee stings you have had in your lifetime. In one instance, I was enjoying a burger at a backyard barbeque. Little did I know that a bee was enjoying my burger, too: a fact I discovered with my next bite. Take my word for it: eating a bee is not advisable. Another incident happened when I was pulling weeds. As I crawled to the next weed patch, my head bumped the dangling birdhouse. The worker bees at the secret hive inside instantly appeared to avenge the bump. Three stings on my cheek were a good enough reason to stop weeding for the day.

Our annoyance with bees seems to be shared in the Old Testament.   Read Deuteronomy 1:44 and Psalm 118:12.   What impression of bees do these verses convey?

12.   Compare this to the scenes in Judges 14:8 and Proverbs 24:13. What value do bees have in these verses?

Sure, honey from bees is important, but more importantly, there are several food favorites which could not be grown without bee pollination. These are: kiwifruit, Brazil nut, watermelon, cantaloupe, squash, pumpkin, gourd, zucchini, and macadamia nuts. Many other plants such as blueberries, avocados and apples are heavily dependent on bees, while not completely critical. So, keeping bees alive in our environment is necessary. [12]

Decline in bee populations in recent decades have been attributed to multiple factors. Certainly changes in the climate and physical environment have had some effect. You may have already heard about the pesticide neonicotinoid. Studies reveal that exposure to this product leaves bees slower to learn, unable to return to their hive, and unable to make the association between floral scents and pollen. These pesticides are systemic, meaning that they affect the entire plant, affect surrounding plants exposed to it through groundwater, plus persist in an environment well past the application period. [13] Although it is not banned in the US, the EPA advises homeowners not to use neonicontid on lawns. [14] There are lesser effects on bee populations from other pesticides also.

Add to this cause the most widespread and destructive infectious agents, viruses: the parasitic mite Varroa Destructor and the fungal agent Nosema. Recent spread of the Asian hornet and the small hive beetle are raising concern. You may have heard about the Asian hornet, also known as "Murder Hornet," which can actually kill an entire hive. It is hoped that its spread into the United States can be stopped. [15]

The Bible primarily associates bees with honey. However, God must have designed bees for their pollination purposes. What would God think about the loss of bee colonies in recent decades? How do you feel about the value of preserving bees? Is there anything we can do to help preserve bees?

Butterflies

13. Besides affecting the bees, neonicotinoids have affected a species we all love: butterflies. With decreasing butterfly populations in California, studies of changes in land use and climate have shown links. Recent findings about bee decline have led scientists to look at this pesticide's effect on butterflies. The correlation is quite strong, as strong as the effect of land conversion. Since use of this pesticide dramatically increased since 1995, it is easy to see the effect on butterfly decline since then. [16] Neonicotinoid is transferred to wildflowers from neighboring agricultural fields treated with this pesticide. Butterflies in the larvae stage are particularly susceptible through their exposure to the contaminated wildflowers, causing death or reduced growth. [17]

Are you ready to join a "Save the Butterfly" campaign? What can we do to help our butterfly populations from declining?

Biodiversity

14. I have found very little explanation in the bible about one very cool reality of nature: the food chain. I am certain that God designed all of creation very specifically: which animals would eat which insects or plants, and which animals would eat those animals, and which would help each other through a symbiotic relationship. In this perfect design each creature lived in the appropriate environment with access to the other creatures in its food chain. Unfortunately, in the many years

since the time of Genesis chapter 1 many of these perfectly conceived food chains have been broken, generally through man's actions.

For example, four out of five species of rhinoceros are endangered or extinct now. Their vegetation diet creates their bulk so that they look particularly yummy for the meat-eating lions. At the same time, they have a symbiotic relationship with many birds. As the rhino roams the plains the oxpecker bird rids it of ticks that are enjoying the rhino's blood.   The rhino's waste products are valuable as soil enrichment. The rhino's food chain relationships happen until ruthless hunters use a tranquilizer gun to stun the animal, then chop off the horn, leaving the rhino to bleed to death. The horns are used in traditional Chinese medicine, but more recently sold for status symbols. With the loss of the rhino species, there is a void in the food chain. [18] [19]

As we hear of land being cleared and burned in the Amazon region, what happens to the plants, insects, birds and animals living there? What happens to these creatures when vast areas are burned by wildfires, or ravaged by floods?

Over 1 billion animals have been killed in the Australian wildfires of 2019. [20]   What happens the next day, the next month, the next year when all of God's perfect food chains there have been disrupted? What happens when rainforest plants we use for medicines no longer exist?

The question is: what does God think about extinctions? What do you think about losing species?

Conclude and Respond
Imagine a warm summer picnic without watermelon. If the current trend in loss of bee population continues, watermelon may not exist in ten years. The same fate may befall cute koala bears, which only exist in the wild in Australia where the incidence of wildfires is increasing. Even more consequential would be the potential starvation of thousands of people in Africa as locusts decimate their crops. But, rather than thinking of this bleak outlook, I suggest you channel your energy into solutions. Look for ways to attract bees to your yard. Look for ways to lessen your contribution to global warming that causes heat waves in Australia. Look for organizations to support which help Africans survive the food loss from the locusts. Ask God to help you to make a difference in any of these pursuits.

Lesson 9 – Action Steps
- Plant bee-friendly and butterfly-friendly plants such as butterfly bush, geraniums, asters, zinnias, crocus, clematis, etc. Search websites for more ideas.
- Use natural pest and weed control in your yard, such as birds and compost.
- Write to lawmakers requesting complete ban of neonicotnoid pesticides in the US, as exists in the E.U.
- Eat less pork to reduce demand and thereby reduce problems with pig waste.

[1] "Extinction of Plants and Animals," Prepared by National Museum of Natural History, Smithsonian Institution, https://naturalhistory.si.edu/education/teaching-resources/paleontology/extinction-over-time)

[2] John R. Platt, "The Faces of Extinction: The Species We Lost in 2019," January 6, 2020, https://therevelator.org/extinction-species-lost-2019/

[3] "Extinction of Plants and Animals," Prepared by National Museum of Natural History.

[4] M. Shahbandeh, "Top 10 U.S. states by inventory of hogs and pigs as of March 2020 (in 1,000s)," April 30, 2020, https://www.statista.com/statistics/194371/top-10-us-states-by-number-of-hogs-and-pigs/

[5] Kendra Pierre-Louis, "Lagoons of Pig Waste Are Overflowing After Florence. Yes, That's as Nasty as It Sounds." The New York Times, September 19, 2018, https://www.nytimes.com/2018/09/19/climate/florence-hog-farms.html

[6] Erin Jordan, "Eight Manure Lagoons Overflow in Western Iowa Because of Flooding," Sioux City Journal, March 26, 2019, https://siouxcityjournal.com/news/state-and-regional/iowa/eight-manure-lagoons-overflow-in-western-iowa-because-of-flooding/article_792b6561-c617-58ea-b287-70c58d3bb2bc.html)

[7] "Numbers of Insects (Species and Individuals)," Prepared by Department of Systematic Biology, Entomology Section, National Museum of Natural History, https://www.si.edu/spotlight/buginfo/bugnos#:~:text=It%20has%20long%20been%20recognized,of%20living%20insects%20are%20known.

[8] Matt McGrath, "Nature Crisis: 'Insect Apocalypse' More Complicated thanThought," BBC News, April 23, 2020, https://www.bbc.com/news/science-environment-52399373#:~:text=Reports%20of%20the%20rapid%20and,caused%20great%20worry%20to%20scientists.&text=The%20compilation%20indicates%20that%20insects,lower%20than%20many%20published%20rates.)

[9] McGrath, "Nature crisis: Insect apocalypse."

[10] "Spotted Lanternfly Alert," prepared by Pennsylvania Department of Agriculture, PA, 2019, https://www.agriculture.pa.gov/Plants_Land_Water/PlantIndustry/Entomology/spotted_lanternfly/SpottedLanternflyAlert/Pages/default.aspx

[11] Abdi Latif Dahir, 'Like an Umbrella Had Covered the Sky': Locust Swarms Despoil Kenya," The New York Times, Feb. 21, 2020, https://www.nytimes.com/2020/02/21/world/africa/locusts-kenya-east-africa.html)

[12] Wikipedia, s.v. " List of Crop Plants Pollinated by Bees," accessed June 2020, https://en.wikipedia.org/wiki/List_of_crop_plants_pollinated_by_bees

[13] F. Muth and A.S.Leonard, " A Neonicotinoid Pesticide Impairs Foraging, But Not Learning, in Free-Flying Bumblebees," Scientific Reports, Nature Research, 2019, https://www.nature.com/articles/s41598-019-39701-5

[14] Britt E. Erickson, "Neonicotinoid Pesticides Can Stay in the US Market, EPA Says," February 3, 2020, https://cen.acs.org/environment/pesticides/Neonicotinoid-pesticides-stay-US-market/98/web/2020/02#:~:text=The%20EPA%20advises%20homeowners%20not,their%20potential%20to%20harm%20bees.

[15] Tiphanie Havard, Marion Laurent, Marie-Pierre Chauzat, "Impact of Stressors on Honey Bees: Some Guidance for Research Emerge from a Meta-Analysis," www.ResearchGate.net , December 20, 2019, https://www.researchgate.net/publication/338090539_Impact_of_Stressors_on_Honey_Bees_Apis_mellifera_Hymenoptera_Apidae_Some_Guidance_for_Research_Emerge_from_a_Meta-Analysis

[16] Michael Foster, et. al., "Increasing Neonicotinoid Use and the Declining Butterfly Fauna of Lowland California," royalsocietypublishing.org, August 1, 2016, https://royalsocietypublishing.org/doi/10.1098/rsbl.2016.0475

[17] Julia Fahrenkamp-Uppenbrink, " Wildflower Contamination with Neonicotinoids," **Science**, April 13, 2018, https://science.sciencemag.org/content/360/6385/167.3#:~:text=Common%20blue%20butterfly%20larvae%20exposed,to%20harmful%20levels%20of%20neonicotinoids.

[18] :"World Animal Day: We Honour Elephant & Rhino," Prepared by Kariega Game Reserve, October 4, 2019, https://www.kariega.co.za/blog/world-animal-day-we-honour-elephant-rhino

[19] Kat Eschner, "Those Little Birds On The Backs Of Rhinos Actually Drink Blood," Smithsonian Magazine, September 22, 2017, https://www.smithsonianmag.com/smart-news/those-little-birds-backs-rhinos-actually-drink-blood-180964912/

[20] Minyvonne Burke, "Video shows koalas, other animals hurt in Australia's fires getting treated," NBC News, January 10, 2020, https://www.nbcnews.com/news/world/video-shows-koalas-other-animals-hurt-australia-s-fires-getting-n1113436

Lesson 10 - God's Vision of the Earth on the Sixth Day: Man - Part 1

I have a hobby: I create landscape scenes out of fabric. Although I enjoy creating these, my main goal is to share them with others. There are many gifted musicians in our church who use their gifts to lead our worship meetings. They are sharing their abilities with others. Perhaps you are a musician like those in my church, or perhaps you have another hobby.   Talents and hobbies are best when shared with other people.

God created our beautiful complex earth. This was not simply for him to look at from on high. He wanted to share his handiwork, thus he created humans. He created the earth for our enjoyment. This is clear from Isaiah 45:18:

> For this is what the Lord says—he who created the heavens, he is God; he who fashioned and made the earth, he founded it; he did not create it to be empty, but formed it to be inhabited...

1.   God says, "Let the Earth bring forth living creatures..." Even though His direction is for the land to bring forth the animals, He is their creator. Look at the description of God's creation of man: "Let us make man in our own image."   Contrast "Earth bring forth creatures," with "...make man in our own image..."   What does this tell you about the intensity of God's involvement in man versus animals?

Genesis tells us that God made man in His own image. What does it mean to you that you are made in God's image?

In God's eyes we are highly valued over the animals. Are there times in your life that you need to remember how valuable you are to God?

Population

2.   In Genesis 1:28a God gives a blessing to man, plus direction to "Be fruitful and multiply and fill the earth..." Today there are many interpretations of "multiply and fill the earth." Does "multiply" mean 2 parents x 1 = 2 children, or 2 parents x 5 = 10 children? What do you personally think this means?

Does "fill the earth" mean that man should inhabit ALL lands? What about lands which are not so fertile such as deserts? Should man be filling those lands?

3.   Have you ever been on a subway in a major city at rush hour?   If so you have experienced train cars so full that you literally cannot move. It takes great effort to extract yourself from the mass of people at your stop. This image signifies the extent of population explosion that has happened in some areas of the world, and could continue to happen if climate change promotes more refugee movements to cooler, inland areas.

There is definitely more room on the earth for man to multiply. The world population as of 2020 is 7.8 billion. If those of child-rearing age "multiply" in one generation, approximately thirty years, the population could be about 10 billion. Is there enough capability to produce food for this population? Also, what happens if warming temperatures truly do cause sea level rise to the effect that island and coastal areas are not inhabitable? What happens if temperatures rise so that Equatorial lands are too hot for man's survival there? If there are climate refugee groups seeking cooler, more sustainable lands, how many people can live in any particular area without causing other kinds of crises?   Even now in 2020 refugee movements have caused political divisions, protests and revolts.

Population growth in Cape Town, South Africa, along with other factors, led to a severe water shortage in 2018. (see "Lesson 3 - God's Vision of the Earth on the Third Day: Water") [1] Population growth in cities in California has contributed to a sizable homeless population. As the population grows, the demand for clean water, food, energy and land increases. As these demands increase, especially in developing countries, environmentally-sound solutions are not readily available. Resources and finances are stretched, often leaving people to suffer and/or starve.

How do you feel about God's direction to Adam and Eve in Genesis 1:28 to "be fruitful and multiply?" Is His instruction to Adam and Eve pertinent to humans living now in the 21st century? What would God want us to do about population growth in cities? What would God want us to do about clean water shortages?

Food Supply
4.   True confessions: I am a food waster; I weigh more than my ideal; I am not a very diligent gardener....Yet...I eat very little meat, at most 2 times per week; I eat several servings of vegetables daily; I try to grow several kinds of vegetables every year.   Because it is time to talk about global food supply, I decided to be honest!

Americans are of the fortunate earth-dwellers who have a good food supply. However, as has been made especially clear with the COVID 19 pandemic, this supply is not necessarily evenly distributed. Unfortunately, some Americans are undernourished. Go a step further to the whole world, and there is an even greater disparity. A look at the numbers shows the stark reality: there are 2 billion people overweight or obese, including 340 million children, while there are 800 million underweight or malnourished. [2] What should we do, first about our nation's food supply problems, then about the worldwide disparities?

5.   Read these three verses to see what the bible says about people in need:

1 Timothy 5:8

1 John 3:17

Acts 20:35

What does God command Christians to do about "neighbors" with food shortages? Do you think God wants us to look at the entire world for this?

6.   The Covid19 Pandemic has put a strain on agricultural production, food processing plants and food shipping processes. Yet, countries, like the United States, with a good resource of suppliers, both domestic and foreign, and efficient means of distribution have fared best. The biggest obstacle to meeting world food needs is the shift to national protectionism, especially during the pandemic. Some economists recommend three needed changes: increased global trade; more efficient and varied production; and a change of diet. [3] Do you think wealthy countries like the USA should be in a "me first" mode, or should they help the developing countries?

7.   In Illinois where I grew up farmers worked their land or raised their cattle on their property which had been in the family for many generations. I am sure God's words to Adam after his disobedience felt pertinent at times:

> Cursed is the ground because of you; through painful toil you will eat food from it all the days of your life. (Genesis 3:17b)

Farming and cattle ranching in the USA have progressed to numerous giant corporate farms, with many automated processes. There are endless fertilizers, pesticides and techniques available to achieve better production. Unfortunately, many areas of the world are way behind the progress made in the US. All of this progress can be stalled with weather events like floods, as seen in the midwest through all of 2019, or like the derecho (hurricane-like storm) which ravaged farmlands and silos in August of 2020.

Some developing countries have moved toward better production. Up to one third of the world's farmland by some estimates has been degraded by poor management or climate change. Techniques are available to reclaim this land for more sustainable use. China has embarked on a program to improve its farmland to a 25% increase in productivity. India has the most arable land spread over different climatic conditions, which through seed adaptation and known techniques could feed more than just its population. What is most needed in the developing nations is investment, either locally or abroad. [4] A similar question: should the United States help struggling countries increase their food production?

8.   John 6:35 says, "Jesus said to them, 'I am the bread of life; whoever comes to me shall not hunger, and whoever believes in me shall never thirst.' " Christians have found this to be true spiritually. What do you, as a Christian, believe God means for physical hunger?   There is the debate about worldwide missions organizations: whether they should address the physical needs of a population first, then teach them about Jesus, or if they should simply teach about Jesus. There are successful missions programs worldwide of both types. Should Christians address food needs first?

Discuss what you believe God desires for missions.

Food Waste

9.   I was astounded to read that agricultural waste/loss accounts for one-third of production. With my gardening "luck" in dealing with pests, I am not surprised that loss due to pests is part of that figure. Loss in harvesting, processing, storage, transportation and consumer food waste account for the remainder. The knowledge for improvement in all areas exists, but, again, simply needs the interest/investment to improve the situation. [5]

In my home I have a few tricks to reduce waste: (a) use masking tape labels for writing dates on leftover containers; (b) serve kids leftovers of an alternate favorite in place of a not-so-favorite-dinner; (c) put remaining lunch-size portions in reheatable containers in the freezer for easy work/school lunch preparation; and (d) using overdue produce in soups, or for addition to the compost pile. In the United States various startup companies are selling "misfits" or "imperfect" produce as a way to reduce waste. How do you handle food waste in your home? Do you ever buy imperfect produce? Name some ways that you could reduce your waste.

Man's Diet

10.   God speaks to man about his diet in Genesis 1:29-30:
    Then God said, "I give you every seed-bearing plant on the face of the whole earth and every tree that has fruit with seed in it. They will be yours for food. And to all the beasts of the earth

and all the birds in the sky and all the creatures that move along the ground—everything that has the breath of life in it—I give every green plant for food." And it was so.

The message is two-part: (a) what man should eat, and (b) what every beast, every bird, everything that creeps on earth and everything that has breath of life should eat.   All creatures would be herbivores, with every green plant for food. Man is directed to eat every plant yielding seed and every tree with seed in its fruit. Thus, God directed the first man and woman on earth to eat as vegetarians. Did you know that? Why do you think God gave the first humans this direction?

How do you classify your eating habits: vegan, vegetarian, pescatarian or meat-eater?

11.   Meat-eaters, heave no fear! Over 1000 years later when Noah emerges after the flood, God changes this direction. Here is Genesis 9:3:
> Everything that lives and moves about will be food for you. Just as I gave you the green plants, I now give you everything.

Bible commentaries explain this change of direction in different ways. The purposes of this study are not about such a question. However, simply consider this: Why do you believe God changes this direction?

12. Did you know that it takes these resources to bring **one pound of beef** to your table: 2,500 gallons of water, 12-16 pounds of grain, 35 pounds of topsoil and the energy equivalent of one gallon of gasoline? Did you know that 70% of US grain production is fed to livestock? [6]

Since meat production uses such a large portion of our resources, the meat-eating trajectory for the increasing population is not sustainable. What if some/most of the US's 70% of agricultural produce which currently feeds cattle was used to feed people? Likewise, could some/most of the 2500 gallons of freshwater needed per pound of beef be used for drinking water?   If we hope, as a world, to be able to meet the increasing food demands of a growing population, we must change our diets. How often do you eat meat: never, once per week, 2-4 times per week, or multiple times per week? Have you tried any beef alternative products such as "Beyond Meat?"   If so, what is your assessment?

13. Have you heard about (excuse me!) "cow farts?" Cows and sheep are ruminant animals, meaning that they release methane when they pass gas. Methane is one of the most potent greenhouse gases, even though its life, about ten years, in the atmosphere is shorter. There are cattle diet changes which may help reduce this problem. Did you know that beef and lamb have the highest emissions per kg, more than double of what others have, such as pork, chicken, eggs? In addition to production costs/emissions, there are costs/emissions associated with fertilizers and pesticides. Think about the amount of grain used for cattle rearing as noted above. The production/distribution of these products uses energy, and, thus, in most cases releases carbon

dioxide. The application of these products releases the greenhouse gas nitrous oxides into the soil, air and water. [7]   (See Lesson 12 - God's Vision of the Earth on the Sixth Day: Man - Part 3)

Knowing the environmental cost of some foods may help people change their diet. Here is a list from highest to lowest for the relative environmental impact based on **emissions** for various proteins:

> lamb, beef, cheese, pork, farmed salmon, turkey, chicken, eggs, peanut butter, nuts, yogurt, dry beans, milk. Lamb and beef generate **more than double** the emissions. [8]

Looking at the cost in terms of **use of land, water, fuel, fertilizer and pesticide**, beef far surpasses all of the others analyzed. Here is the hierarchy from highest to lowest in environmental costs:

> beef, chicken, eggs, almonds, kidney beans. [9]

Does knowing about the COST of beef production cause you to reconsider that burger? Perhaps in the future market/government trends may influence our meat choices for the better of our planet. Do you think governments could affect citizens' diets?

Subdue Command

14.   Many Bible versions use the word, "subdue," however the Contemporary English version and the Good New Translation state, "bring it under your control." Man's control of the earth has been evidenced in using the land for agriculture, ranching, entertainment and energy production. Also, man has subdued the earth by using natural resources for building materials for skyscrapers and roadways. Name ways that man has "subdued the earth" for (a) good purposes and (b) harmful purposes.

15.   In Genesis 1:28 God also commanded man to have dominion over....all the earth and every living thing. One dictionary definition for dominion is: supreme authority.   List what you believe man should have "supreme authority" over.

What is our heavenly father's method for dominion over us? Think of His laws, His guidance, His actions.

Genesis tells us that God made man in His own image. If we are made in God's image, in what manner should we have dominion over the earth? Can we operate as the supreme authority while we are behaving as God would?

16.   Note that God not only directs man to be fruitful and multiply, but He creates plants that are seed-bearing and trees with seed in its fruit. God wants the plants and trees to be fruitful and multiply. Likewise, He wants the birds, fish and animals to be fruitful and multiply. He wants all of

these to continue to exist on earth.   What activities of humans have helped to maintain this part of God's plan? What activities of humans do not help maintain this part of God's plan?

After Adam's and Eve's Sin

17.   Human beings are made in God's image. That means we have greater mental ability than any animal. We have freedom to make choices everyday. However, because of Adam's and Eve's original sin of eating from the tree of the knowledge of good and evil, man can use those higher abilities inappropriately. History has shown that poor choices can be disastrous.

Fortunately, God has given us further guidance for good choices in the Bible. What are your favorite verses for His guidance?   What techniques do you use to help guide your everyday choices?

Some Statistics

18.   Have you heard about the energy consumption of the United States? I must admit I am a bit embarrassed that we have the highest per person consumption in the world. Here is a chart I prepared to compare[10]:

Entity	Percent of world population	Percent of world's energy consumption
United States	> 5%	17%
European Union	7%	11%
China	18%	24%

I am equally unhappy about the predictions for the United States' energy sources: Unless changes are made, by 2050 79% will come from fossil fuels. Renewable energy production is only expected to rise at a rate of 1.9% annually between 2019 and 2050. It is sad to learn that methane leakage from gas and oil fracking and pipelines accounts for 2.3 % of the US annual natural gas production. I ask, why can this not be better controlled? [11]   Unfortunately, the current administration removed the methane leakage limits on oil and gas production in August 2020. Thus, fossil fuel companies no longer have to repair leaks. Scientists predict that, since the methane is 84 times as potent than carbon dioxide, the ongoing leaks may undo much progress that has been made with carbon reduction. [12]

How do you feel about the US having the highest per person energy consumption? How do you feel about the federal government reducing regulations?

Toilet Paper Impact

19.   Did you realize that Americans, who represent 4% of the world's population, use 20% of the world's toilet tissue?   Why do you think there is a disparity in American use of toilet paper compared to the world?

Toilet paper certainly seems like a necessity about which you could do little to change environmental impact. Trees are cut down, the wood pulp is extracted, then processed using water, bleach and energy. The manufacturing process for one roll requires 37 gallons of water in addition to the energy and emissions cost for tree harvest, production and shipping.

As you could guess, the impact is greater with use of virgin pulp (from trees) than with use of recycled material. For example, if the paper you are writing on is recycled into toilet paper, less energy, less water and less bleach would be required, plus the carbon-absorbing tree would not be destroyed. [13] For all environmental costs, using recycled materials means saving: 712 million trees, one-half of the water, and one-third of the energy. [14]

The bleaching process was revised in the mid-1990s to use less elemental bleach. The elemental bleach process released dioxins which cause cancer, birth defects, diabetes and allergies. The process used since then is better, but may still release harmful chlorine gas.   Our best defense for this is to use recycled materials, which in most cases has been bleached in its first life and requires much less for its second life. The label TCF - Totally Chlorine Free means that no chlorine was used. How could we consumers influence manufacturers to use less chlorine?

Another TP option is to use products that are more sustainable, like tree-free paper products. I have been purchasing tree-free bamboo products for a few years now. My skeptical friends were surprised at its soft feel when I gave each a sample piece. Other sustainable sources are: agricultural waste, kenaf (alternative fibre) and wheat straw.   These should be checked for impact through organizations like Roundtable on Sustainable Biomaterials.

Have you ever tried tree-free paper products? Have you ever used a bidet?

Other Paper Products

20. Have you ever used a real handkerchief?   Do you use paper towels for cleaning, or old fabric rags? Ever since I had my first apartment after college **(many** years ago!), I have been using only cloth napkins, cloth kitchen towels and cloth cleaning rags. Perhaps my mom was the best example to me for this environmentally responsible approach. So, it was logical that I would follow her steps in use of cloth diapers for my two children. (This helps with potty-training, as suggested to me from my mother-in-law!) It was easy for me to think of my children's future life on earth as I pinned on the cloth diapers. I dare say that my use of these had to be far easier with our modern machines than my mother labored thorough with a wringer washer and no dryer. By now you think I am about 100 years old!

Have you "come a long way" by following trends with disposable diapers, paper plates and swiffer mops? How often do you need to replenish these supplies? Have you thought about using reusable alternatives?

Conclude and Respond

In six days God created the Earth in all of its magnificence and intricacy. All of the components of our planet "home" were completed before God created humans. Knowing this should help us realize the value that God puts in us. In addition, God directed man to have dominion over the earth. In fact, He gave man a brain in order to do this better than any other animal. Through this week focus on the abilities God has given you. Express your thankfulness to Him in your daily prayers.

Lesson 10 – Action Steps

- Buy imperfect produce.
- Eliminate food waste in your home.
- Replace use of disposable paper products at home with cloth napkins, towels, cleaning rags, and/or buy recycled and renewably-produced products.
- Write to lawmakers to support assistance to developing countries with sustainable farming practices.
- Write to lawmakers to request stronger limits and enforcement of methane leaks in gas production.

[1] Krista Mahr, "How Cape Town Was Saved From Running Out Of Water," The Guardian, May 4, 2018, https://www.theguardian.com/world/2018/may/04/back-from-the-brink-how-cape-town-cracked-its-water-crisis

[2] Iain Marlow and Agnieszka de Sousa, "What It Will Take to Avoid a Global Food Shortage," Bloomburg.com, June 9, 2020, https://www.bloomberg.com/graphics/2020-solving-the-global-food-problem/

[3] Marlow and de Sousa, "What It Will Take."

[4] Marlow and de Sousa, "What It Will Take."

[5] Marlow and de Sousa, "What It Will Take."

[6] "Food Choices and the Planet," Prepared by Earthsave.org, accessed July 2020, https://www.earthsave.org/environment.htm

[7] "Meat Eaters Guide Report: Climate and Environmental Impacts, 2011," Prepared by Environmental Working Group, https://www.ewg.org/meateatersguide/a-meat-eaters-guide-to-climate-change-health-what-you-eat-matters/climate-and-environmental-impacts/

[8] "Meat Eaters Guide," Prepared by Environmental Working Group.

[9] J. Sabate, et al, "The Environmental Cost of Protein Food Choices," Cambridge Core, Cambridge.org, August 2015 , https://www.cambridge.org/core/journals/public-health-nutrition/article/environmental-cost-of-protein-food-choices/DB40E5C12D662913CC342D3C19F85F7D/core-reader#

[10] "U.S. ENERGY SYSTEM FACTSHEET," Prepared by Center for Sustainable Systems, University of Michigan, 2020, http://css.umich.edu/factsheets/us-energy-system-factsheet

[11] "U.S. ENERGY SYSTEM FACTSHEET," Prepared by Center for Sustainable Systems.

[12] Coral Davenport, "Trump Eliminates Major Methane Rule, Even as Leaks Are Worsening," The New York Times, August 20, 2020, https://www.nytimes.com/2020/08/13/climate/trump-methane.html

[13] Jennifer Skene, "The Issue With the Tissue," National Resource Defense Council, February 2019, https://www.nrdc.org/sites/default/files/issue-tissue-how-americans-are-flushing-forests-down-toilet-report.pdf

[14] "Environmental Impact of Toilet Paper," Prepared by The World Counts, 2020, https://www.theworldcounts.com/challenges/consumption/other-products/environmental-impact-of-toilet-paper/story

Lesson 11: God's Vision of the Earth on the Sixth Day: Man - Part 2

Do you believe that God would have wanted mankind to have as many diseases as we do? I do not believe so. Doctors understand the origins of most diseases, and fortunately many cures. Still, some people do die from their illnesses. From an earthly perspective it is quite difficult to lose a loved one, even with believing in a reunion in eternal life. The absence of his or her physical presence is perhaps only relieved through a reliance on God, and on friends and relatives. Unfortunately, our earth's population density and the condition of earth's environment seem to have promoted some diseases.

1.   Disease is certainly part of the bible. In both the Old and New Testaments God, Jesus and the disciples heal people of their afflictions. Read these verses:

    Deuteronomy 7:15

    Matthew 9:35

    Matthew 10:1

In contrast, there are times that God is on the opposite side. Read and make note of why you believe God acted as He did. :

    Deuteronomy 28:15-22

    2Chronicles 21:12-15

    Jeremiah 8:19b - 22

2.   The bible teaches that Christians have the promise of eternal life. So, with that in mind, are not suffering and diseases of no significance? Read what Romans 8:18 says:
> For I consider that the sufferings of this present time are not worth comparing with the glory that is to be revealed to us.

What do you believe about our current suffering? How do you feel about the image of God as the healer? Do you believe He will heal any Christians?

Diseases

3.   As I sit to write about the environmental impact of diseases, the official count of deaths in the USA from COVID 19 is now over 200,000, while that in the world is over 950,000. The tremendous loss of life is horrendous. For purposes of this book, it could be valuable to look at the origin of the virus, the origin lessons for future pandemics and safeguards for environmental factors.

COVID19 is one of several current diseases which originated in animals. A zoonotic pathogen jumps from the animal to a human through food, water, the environment or direct contact. Similar diseases are rabies, Lymes disease, Ebola, and, in its original transmission, HIV. Human contact with animals is unavoidable, especially considering the various possible transmission paths.

What could help are standards worldwide for clean drinking water, waste removal, and animal care. In the United States we are fortunate to have such standards enforced, but this should be a priority worldwide. Leadership in developing countries should provide education about ways to prevent spread.   Also, animals raised for our food are commonly treated with antibiotics. This practice could encourage drug-resistant zoonotic pathogens to infect animal and human populations, and, thus, requires further study. The One Health approach coordinates efforts of several worldwide organizations for identification, prevention and control of animal diseases. [1]

Have you or your family been affected with COVID 19? Have you been affected by any similar diseases: Lymes disease, rabies, HIV?

4. In the bible leprosy was a common illness. Because of its contagion, an unusual command was given in Numbers 5:2:

> Command the people of Israel that they put out of the camp everyone who is leprous or has a discharge and everyone who is unclean through contact with the dead.

This command does not differ from some of the quarantine restrictions that have been set for COVID 19. What guidelines have been set by your government? How do you feel about these guidelines? How do you feel about protests against the rules?

What is your source for information about such diseases?

Other Diseases

5.   Climate-related factors such as heavy rainfall, flooding, warmer temperatures can impact the prevalence of diseases. These factors can cause contamination of food and water, and the spread of insect-borne diseases. Developing countries with less sophisticated infrastructure face a more severe problem. For example, cholera cases increased in Bangladesh during periods of high or low rainfall.

Similar diseases there saw surges with higher temperatures and rainfall events: the mosquito-borne diseases of malaria, dengue fever and Japanese encephalitis. Heavy rainfall and flooding in Australia have caused outbreaks of two mosquito-borne diseases: Murray Valley encephalitis and Ross River fever. Canada, Sweden and the Czech Republic have experienced increased tick-borne diseases simultaneously with the higher temperatures of global warming. [2] What do you think governments and citizens can do to limit the spread of diseases?   Do you believe that countries such as the United States have any obligation to help developing countries reduce the spread of infectious diseases?

6.   In addition, habitat changes are consequential for disease spread. In my area of the US suburban development has relocated and/or increased deer population, and likely the spread of lyme disease. Have you experienced any similar changes in your area?   What could be done about these situations which exacerbate disease spread?

Plastics

7.   Can you name all of the plastics you use in one month?   Hold on - I feel like this should be a competition. Ask a friend to make a list, too. Two minutes. Ready, set, go!

> My list: Water bottles, soda bottles, store bags, plastic kitchen bags, trash bags, milk carton, lunchmeat wrapper, bread wrapper, condiments' jars, sandwich bags, vinyl lunch box, vinyl ice packs, refillable water bottle, plastic pens, tape, plastic mechanical pencils, laptop housing, USB cord for mouse, flash drive, CDs, toothbrush, toothpaste tube, car key Fob, car door handles, car dashboard, drink holders…

How many did you get in two minutes?

8.   Most of these are a "given" part of life now, but does it really have to be like this:

> I buy a new mouse for my computer. The store wants to put the package in a plastic bag bearing their name, but I decline. At home I eagerly begin the ten-minute process to un-package it: The outside layer of hard plastic needs to be cut with a strong scissors in a few directions in order to release the inside package. The plastic encasing the mouse itself needs to be pried on one side in order to free the mouse. The attached cord was apparently threatening to escape, too, so it has its own plastic package. Once I have carefully cut this package, I can unwrap the plastic-coated wire twist-tie. Finally I can plug in the plastic USB to continue writing this book.

How did we get to this?

9.   Early versions of plastics were first developed in the late 1800s, culminating with the first real synthetic, mass-produced plastic, called Bakelite, in 1907 by Leo Baekeland. The key ingredient in all plastics is crude oil. It is refined, separated into fractions, of which the naphtha fraction is used for plastic. Once in that state, it can be formed into whatever gadget or type of packaging is desired. [3]
There is a downside for all of the convenience of plastic. Plastic is not biodegradable.That is, it never breaks down. So, any plastic disposed of in a trash bag, tossed on a roadside, dumped in a lake, or floated into the ocean will ALWAYS be in the condition it is now. It is likely that this foreign object will have some effect on its "habitat." It may entrap a fish, hurt or kill a creature that eats it, clog a drainage ditch, or simply accumulate to become a mountainous landfill. But, perhaps the user could put the plastic into recycling, and prevent all of these problems. What really happens to that plastic recycling?

Plastic Recycling

10. We were fooled! Remember the days when we paid the deposit for soda bottles, then diligently brought them back to the store to recoup it. We felt so good that these plastics may soon become playground surfaces, picnic tables, or even new plastic bottles.

Perhaps the economics were never in favor of recycling plastics, despite public relations to the contrary. An investigation by NPR and PBS Frontline uncovered the fallacious campaign of the plastics industry. If they hoped to get consumers to "buy in" to plastic as a replacement for glass, metal and wood packaging and products, they would have to sell it as having similar life cycles. Americans who were already collecting their newspapers, glass and tin cans, were pleased when plastic containers appeared on the market, to hear that these, too, could be recycled. In hindsight, we should have suspected some slight of hand when plastics needed to be separated by codes, with many being relegated to the trash can.

In fact a 1974 speech by an industry insider voiced the reality, "There is serious doubt that [recycling plastic] can ever be made viable on an economic basis. " [4]   In contrast, the plastics industry itself has certainly been economically viable with profits of billions of dollars.
An industry ad from 1990 shows this marvelous plastic bottle:

> "The bottle may look empty, yet it's anything but trash," says one ad from 1990 showing a plastic bottle bouncing out of a garbage truck. "It's full of potential. ... We've pioneered the country's largest, most comprehensive plastic recycling program to help plastic fill valuable uses and roles. [5]

With this ad rolling on all American TVs, executives acknowledged in secret that the collection, sorting, processing into a lesser product, which after one or two cycles would be landfill-bound, was far too costly. This was the exact truth, especially in light of the minimal cost of new plastic. [6]

How do you feel about being misled by the plastics industry? Have you been concerned that a substantial amount of the plastics we use everyday cannot go into the recycling bin? Does your town still collect plastics for recycling?

Plastic Pollution

11.   A few years ago all of the talk was about the six-pack plastic rings floating in the ocean, strangling fish. I admit that I was puzzled, since I rarely, if ever, saw anyone at the beach toss one into the waves. I discovered that much of the ocean plastic had been inappropriately disposed of anywhere, then was carried by the wind or water to streams, rivers and oceans.

Once the plastics are in the ocean, sunlight, waves and salt water break much of it down into small microplastics (5 mm or less). From the referenced study it has been estimated that there are 5.25 trillion of these particles, weighing 270,000 tons in the oceans. Ocean currents send them around the world, sometimes circling around in the gyres (see "Lesson 3 - God's Vision of the Earth on the Third Day: Water" - "Ocean Currents"). Since they are not biodegradable, they float,...and float,...and float, all the while attaching to pollutants like flame retardants and industrial chemicals. Hungry fish gulp the plastic-filled water and eat plastic-filled smaller fish. Next thing you know the toxin-coated plastics are in the fish on our dinner plates.[7]

Specific areas with large concentrations of these particles have been identified in the oceans. Have you heard of the Great Pacific Garbage Patch? Approximately 705,000 tons of plastic particles and other garbage are stuck in two areas of the North Pacific Subtropical Gyre (see gyres in "Ocean Currents" in Third Day lesson), which are near Japan and between Hawaii and the US west coast. Other trash, such as fishing nets, shoes, or any trans-Pacific cargo item, has likely come from ships or runoff from the coasts. This material floats with the plastic soup, until up to 70% of it sinks to the ocean floor. Since the plastics are not biodegradable, they will remain there forever, continually being supplemented with more of our waste. [8]

Scientists estimate that, following current trends, there would be more plastic than fish in the oceans by 2050. These particles also absorb toxic and carcinogenic pollutants, eventually harming marine life and human consumers.[9]

Did you know about these plastics? What do you think could be done to stop plastics from filling the ocean?

12.   Unfortunately, the problem doesn't end there. There are plastic particles in our atmosphere. A study published in June 2020 in the journal, Science, reported evidence of plastics in 98% of the 339 samples collected from parks in the western United States. The quantities found translate to 1000 tons of tiny fragments raining down annually just in the tested areas. Where do these come from? Rain and snow carry larger particles probably from nearby urban areas, whereas smaller particles are likely carried in atmospheric air currents from more distant areas.

Because the air already carries other particles, such as the more harmful black carbon in soot, the concentration of plastics is relatively small at this time. However, higher concentrations found in indoor office spaces have been linked to lung disease and tissue damage. The World Health Organization estimated that small particulate pollution caused 4.2 million deaths worldwide in 2016. [10]   Additional studies will help determine the health impact of the plastics. (I wonder if Covid19 face masks will keep plastics out of our lungs?) Do ever hear of air quality alerts in your area? If so, where is the pollution coming from?

13.   God must be so disappointed with man. Not only have we created plateaus of trash landfills, but we have also been sending our beloved plastics into the oceans and the air. The waters He created are warmer, more acidic, and now we find out, are filled with minute plastics. His perfectly-balanced atmosphere has tipped the scales with the extra gases we have added, but is also infiltrated with harmful particles.

Perhaps a look at a few of the Ten Commandments may help us understand how we got here. Look up and write down these three which I believe have pertinence:

(1)

(2)

(10)

I am preaching to myself now, too: is it possible that our eyes, our desires, our hearts, our spirits are not always pointed in the right direction? Do we ever put our materialism above "the Lord, thy God?" Can idols and things we covet be made of plastic?

14.   How do we get out of this crazy plastic black hole we are in? There are a number of actions we can take personally:

- If you have children or grandchildren, live the truth that spending time with the child is more valuable than a gift of a plastic toy.
- Assure that you dispose of plastic containers properly.
- Pack your purchases in reusable cloth bags or paper bags.
- Choose products that are in glass containers, which are much more likely to be recycled.
- When only plastic containers are available, buy the largest quantity. There is less packaging per ounce in larger containers.
- When possible buy products in refillable plastic containers.
- Purchase products made with 100% recycled material, such as trash bags.
- Look for biodegradable plastics, even though their recycling process is complex. Improvements are being made with these all of the time.
- Be a wise consumer who will pay more for a more durable plastic product rather than buying a cheaper one which could break more easily.
- Write letters to companies encouraging their use of other-than-plastic packaging and discouraging redundant layers of packaging.

Are there any of these actions that you currently take? Are you inspired to begin to do any of the above?

Recycling

15. Can you recall when your family first started recycling? Was it with the bottle deposit paid to the store, to be returned for refund? Or, maybe tying the newspapers with string for curbside pickup? These limited recycling efforts evolved to filling multiple buckets for different types of items. Now our pickup allows "single stream" with all types in one container.

I was surprised to hear about the process at our county recycling facility from my friend whose son worked there: several employees monitor a belt as the truck contents flowed by. They were tasked with removing undesirables, including any container with food traces. So, all of my years of fast-rinsing bottles probably yielded only 50% of my refuse moving to the recycling phase. How thoroughly do you rinse your recycling?

16. It was also enlightening to hear a few years later that he lost his job due to (his explanation) "China not accepting much of our recycling." For many years we had a market, meager as it was, with China for our recycling. Then, in 2018 the US administration imposed tariffs on many Chinese imports. As long as those ships were sending far fewer products to the US, there were far fewer ships making the return trip to carry our recyclables there.   There have been a few smaller replacement markets, but other factors have inhibited the process. These are:

    a.   Low oil prices mean that new "virgin plastic" is cheaper than recycled plastic.

    b.   Plastics degrade more through each recycle, leaving less strength for the final product. This is not true for glass or metal, for which recycling is more feasible.

    c.   It is cheaper for towns to incinerate the plastics than to recycle them: The town of Franklin, NH, is being charged $125 a ton to recycle, versus $68 a ton to incinerate. So, most towns would choose to incinerate, releasing toxins, mercury, lead and carbon into the air, rather than pay more.

    d.   Some towns have chosen to dump the recycling into landfills. However, organic waste in a landfill decomposes, emitting methane into our atmosphere. Recall that methane is a much more potent greenhouse gas. Should I mention the cost of shipping to landfills, and the increasing need for landfill space?

    e.   Sadly, some cities and towns no longer collect recycling for these reasons. [11]

How much of your waste goes into your recycling bin? Did you ever realize that much of the recycling doesn't get recycled?   What can you do to help the recycling problem?

17. Unfortunately, some of our recycling that makes it onto ships is incinerated in India, Indonesia and other countries. The lower grade plastics are sorted out and given to locals as an energy resource. In Indonesia, plastic burning for fuel for tofu production creates a serious pollution problem.

In fact, a council of four independent environmental groups presented findings to the government in Indonesia in December 2019. The study reported widespread food, air and water contamination by dioxin, mercury and lead. Dioxin is known to cause cancer, birth defects and Parkinson's disease. Government regulations are not strictly enforced, as any action resulting from this report would not be, due to the economic cost. Indonesia's plans to build four waste -to-energy incinerators, with only five-year monitoring, are under scrutiny. [12]   Does the United States have any responsibility to monitor what happens to our recycling sent to other countries?

18. Purchasing Recycled Products   - Have you seen the terms "Pre-consumer" and "Post-consumer" recycling?   Picture a stack of copy paper.   You use much of it to print bank statements, then eventually years later put these in recycling. This would be called, "Post-Consumer Recycling." Perhaps when you are printing these a blank page gets into the pile occasionally, then gets added to the recycling pile years later. These blank pages are technically, "Pre-Consumer Recycling," since they were never "used" by the consumer.   Manufacturing firms may create pre-consumer recycling from printer over-runs, misprints, obsolete stock or trimmed edges. So, which type do you think would have less environmental cost?   The post-consumer kind would because it did serve a purpose in its life before it was recycled. [13]

(Note that this idea applies to food waste also, since the banana peel of a banana which you have eaten is less costly than the peel of a rotten banana that was never eaten. The peel from the good banana is post-consumer and the rotten banana peel is pre-consumer. So, eat your bananas on time!)

Fortunately, there are various sources for "recycled" products now. I always buy the recycled copy paper for our printer, plus recycled plastic garbage bags. The impediments for the general population are that many of these products have not yet appeared in their local stores, plus, the recycled product is almost always more expensive. Should our government place a higher tax on items that are not recycled or not made of renewable materials? Do you, or would you buy a more expensive item that is made of recycled or sustainable materials?

Conclude and Respond
Look around you this week to do an honest assessment of the amount of plastics in your home. Pray about what you should do to reduce your plastic consumption.
Also, based on Numbers 5:2 (question #4 above), think about the rules and/or recommendations being given concerning Covid 19. Or, if you are reading this years later, when this disease is no longer prevalent in the world, consider what is the public's responsibility to both be aware and be cooperative in times of disease outbreak. Pray that God would direct our leaders for the best outcome.

<u>**Lesson 11 – Action Steps**</u>
- Give the gift of "Time spent with child" rather than a plastic toy.
- Choose products in glass jars instead of plastic whenever possible. If no glass option, buy larger container for less per-measure packaging.
- Thoroughly clean plastics for recycling to assure their acceptance for recycling.
- Buy products made with 100% recycled materials.

[1] "Zoonoses," Prepared by World Health Organization, July 29, 2020,   https://www.who.int/news-room/fact-sheets/detail/zoonoses

[2] Ichiro Kurane, "The Effect of Global Warming on Infectious Diseases," National Center for Biotechnology Information, U.S. National Library of Medicine, December 7, 2010,
https://www.ncbi.nlm.nih.gov/pmc/articles/PMC3766891/#:~:text=Thus%2C%20the%20levels%20of%20the,%2C%20and%20tick%2Dborne%20encephalitis.

[3] "Plastics Pollution," Prepared by Conference Series, accessed August 2020,
https://pollution.conferenceseries.com/events-list/plastic-pollution

[4] Laura Sullivan, "How Big Oil Misled The Public Into Believing Plastic Would Be Recycled," National Public Radio, September 11,2020, https://www.npr.org/2020/09/11/897692090/how-big-oil-misled-the-public-into-believing-plastic-would-be-recycled

[5] Sullivan, "How Big Oil Misled."

[6] Sullivan, "How Big Oil Misled."

[7] "The Truth About Recycling" prepared by 5 Gyres Science to Solutions, 5Gyres.org, accessed September 2020,
https://www.5gyres.org/truth-about-recycling

[8] Jeannie Evers and Caryl-Sue, "Great Pacific Garbage Patch," National Geographic Society, July 5, 2019,
https://www.nationalgeographic.org/encyclopedia/great-pacific-garbage-patch/

[9] Arn Baker, "Plastics Still Manage to Reach the End of the World," Time Magazine, April 9, 2020,
https://time.com/5818225/microplastics-antartica/#:~:text=An%20estimated%208%20million%20metric,in%20the%20ocean%20by%202050.

[10] John Schwartz, " Plastic? It's Everywhere, Even in the Air We Breathe, Scientists Report," The New York Times, June 12, 2020, p. A 16.

[11] Alana Semuels, "Is This the End of Recycling?," The Atlantic, March 5, 2019,
https://www.theatlantic.com/technology/archive/2019/03/china-has-stopped-accepting-our-trash/584131/)

[12] Richard C. Paddock, "Indonesia Lets Plastic Burning Continue Despite Warning on Toxins," The New York Times, Dec. 19, 2019   https://www.nytimes.com/2019/12/19/world/asia/indonesia-dioxin-plastic-tofu.html)

[13] Jennifer Skene, "The Issue With the Tissue," National Resource Defense Council, February 2019,
https://www.nrdc.org/sites/default/files/issue-tissue-how-americans-are-flushing-forests-down-toilet-report.pdf

Lesson 12: God's Vision of the Earth on the Sixth Day: Man - Part 3

Perhaps you feel as I do that there is such beauty in our natural world. Whether you live in a rural area or a city I hope that you are able to experience nature's inspiration. However, our earth has regrettably been subject to man's poor practices and negligent "improvements," so as to leave a dirtied environment. This verse from Proverbs 25:26 (ESV) speaks of pollution:

Like a muddied spring or a polluted fountain is a righteous man who gives way before the wicked.

Looking at "a righteous man who gives way before the wicked," gives the image of a sinner. So, does a "muddied spring" or "polluted fountain" imply sin? Has the man who has muddied a spring or polluted water sinned? Consider these questions as you work through this lesson.

1. Let us review God's direction to man as expressed in Psalm 8:6-8 (ESV):

    You have given him dominion over the works of your hands; you have put all things under his feet, all sheep and oxen, and also the beasts of the field, the birds of the heavens, and the fish of the sea, whatever passes along the paths of the seas.

Since many churches express different ideas about "dominion," what do you think this term implies? Should there be any "limitation" about how much man can dominate nature?

2. As is often the case in the bible, in the New Testament there is further direction about the "dominion" idea. Read Luke 12: 48b (ESV):

    Everyone to whom much was given, of him much will be required, and from him to whom they entrusted much, they will demand the more.

This seems to demand man's accountability to God. Do you believe that man has accountability for his actions, his "dominion?" If so, do you believe that man has accountability for taking care of the earth which God has given to him?

Pollution

3.   When I was a child my family had an "ash pit" in the backyard. Every day one of us had to carry our trash out there, then dad would set the trash on fire.   This "ash pit" was a concrete base, with concrete block walls on three sides. This method was used by many of the town residents, since there was no garbage pick up. Not only that, there were no plastic trash bags. There were no plastic bags for packing your purchases from stores, no plastic parts in anything. Our weekly grocery supplies for our family of eight were loaded in the car in paper bags or no bags. While burning trash has environmental costs in the emissions (carbon dioxide and PAH particulate matter, which is polycyclic aromatic hydrocarbons), living without all of the plastic products was perhaps more beneficial for our environment. In addition there are numerous benefits to not having emissions from waste management trucks and pollution from landfills.

Perhaps the greatest pollution concern is the introduction of man-made chemicals in our environment. From 1930 to 2000 the world's chemical production increased 400 times. These chemicals have changed our lives, sometimes for the better and sometimes for the worst. Our greatest concern is for these three types: those that persist and accumulate in the environment (ex. DDT, chlordane in pesticides), those which cause cancer or damage DNA (ex. soot, asbestos, cigarette smoke chemicals) and those that disrupt hormones and the endocrine system in humans (ex.pesticides like Organochlorines and Phenylamide fungicides).

Several years ago we were all afraid to eat tuna and shellfish due to mercury levels. I will use this dilemma to explain how the level of toxins can vary. All fish and animals have the potential for exposure to metals and toxins in water, air and food sources. Certainly the danger depends on the specific pollutant, so I will focus on one, mercury.

Out in the ocean the very young tuna eats tiny zooplankton, containing little or no methylmercury (the form of mercury which pollutes bodies of water). As they grow small tuna fish eat other smaller fish, krill or sardines. Each of the smaller prey may have absorbed a small amount of methylmercury before being eaten. As the tuna grows larger, it eats shrimp, lobsters and shad, each of which absorbs more methylmercury. By the time Chicken of the Sea tuna company catches your tuna lunch, it has a high level of methylmercury toxin. What has happened is called biomagnification. Animals higher in the food chain have accumulated toxins at higher levels, with greater effects for human consumers.[1] Biomagnification applies to all pollutants, for all parts of our food supply.

Methylmercury can cause permanent damage to the brain and spinal cord. It is particularly harmful to the central nervous system of unborn babies and infants, although high concentrations in adults have some repercussions. Being a vegetarian is looking even better!

How can you avoid the ill effects of pollution? What role should governments play in regulating pollutants?

Air Pollution

4.   The closest I have come to breathing in air pollution (that I know of) is while cleaning the shower stall. Has this happened to you: when it *seems* that the only "air" entering your lungs is chlorine bleach?   Perhaps you have experienced air pollution exposure from a fire, city smog or chemicals at work. The bible paints a vivid picture of air pollution in <u>Exodus 9:10</u>:

> So they took soot from a furnace and stood before Pharaoh. Moses tossed it into the air,
> and festering boils broke out on people and animals.

God used this skin affliction as one of the plagues against Egypt. The image matches that of soot in the air from wildfires, or emissions from a factory. Do you think that when God directed Moses to use the furnace soot He pictured what humans could do to fill our air?   How far have we strayed from God's design?

5.   Currently 7 million deaths annually are attributed to air pollution. The most common air pollution culprits, nitrogen oxide, sulfur oxide and ozone, enter the body as gases or particulate matter. Minute particulate matter, as in soot, causes the most damage to the lungs, and, thus, raises the air quality alerts. Harmful ground-level ozone is formed from nitrogen oxide, hydrocarbons (volatile organic compounds) and sunlight. All of these culprits penetrate the lungs, affecting the respiratory (breathing) and vascular (blood flow) systems, causing or intensifying: asthma, cancer, high blood pressure, pulmonary diseases and heart disease.[2]   Have you been exposed to air pollution, smoke or smog? Do you have any of these illnesses?

6.   All fossil fuel-burning activities release carbon dioxide, sulfur dioxide, nitrous oxide, volatile organic compounds(VOCs) and particulates. The primary source for sulfur dioxide is coal-fired power plants, whereas nitrogen oxide's largest source is vehicle exhaust.   Wildfires emit nitrogen oxide, visible as the reddish brown smog, and particulate matter. You may have heard about the air quality alerts during the extensive fires on the US west coast in 2020. [3]

In some areas of the world air pollution has been decreased and controlled through regulations. In the United States from 1995 to 2019, annual emissions of sulfur dioxide fell 92%, while nitrogen oxide fell 85%. Even with these favorable results, a common political debate concerns environmental regulation versus business development. [4]

However, in many areas of the world there are fewer regulations and even less monitoring. This has been the case in Brazil, with the fires in their rainforest over recent years (2018-2020). Brazil's president chose to limit enforcement until international pressure incited some action. India has the distinction, based on the 2018 World Air Quality Report, of having seven out of the worst ten cities, and 22 out of the worst 30 cities in the world for pollution. Its government has set the goal for 40% of renewable energy by 2030, but the prevalence of coal-powered plants keeps the emissions high. [5]

How do you feel about government regulation of pollutants? What if you knew that the regulations raise the price of products?

Water Pollution

7.   Several months ago we received a notice from our municipal water provider stating that recent testing prescribed "further treatment" of our water. The notice proceeded to convey the hope that this would be a temporary measure. Such action only happens in the United States because of government regulation and monitoring of water supplies. I do believe we are fortunate. Many countries around the world have little regulation or enforcement. In addition many areas do not have "municipal water providers," but rely on wells or nearby streams and rivers.

Freshwater is critical for human life: for drinking, for cooking, for bathing, for fish, for animals, for birds and for food production. Eighty percent of the world's wastewater is not adequately treated, polluted with animal and human waste, toxic industrial discharge, agricultural fertilizers and pesticides, pharmaceutical discharge, and physical trash, including plastics. You can likely recall an oil spill event in recent history, complete with an image of birds struggling to move with oil-laden wings. Oil spills or any other water pollution, are less diffused and, thus, more potent, in still water like lakes and ponds. In moving water the pollutant becomes more diffused, but also more widespread. [6]

Do you know where your local water supply originates, i.e. a reservoir? Have you ever heard from your municipal water provider about necessary water treatment changes? Do you believe wealthy nations should help poor nations achieve a better water supply, or should this continue to be improved through NGOs (non-governmental organizations)?

Pollution from PFOs and PFOAs

8.   Do you use non-stick pans? Do you have carpet? Do you use cosmetics? Do you use paint? If you answered "yes," to any of these, did you know that they contain perfluoroalkyl substances? These chemical compounds deter water and grease, and thereby, are quite valuable in some of our everyday products. Once they are in a human body, they bind to proteins for many years. Recent studies on animals have revealed many potential problems for humans: thyroid dysfunctions, delayed puberty, osteoarthritis, increased levels of uric acid, liver problems, cholesterol changes and immune disorders. High levels of the PFOs and PFOAs in humans may cause skeletal issues, cardiovascular problems, testicular, kidney or thyroid cancer. [7]

Studies have identified avenues for greatest exposure. Drinking water or food can be contaminated with these. Food contamination can result from packaging with these substances, or from soil contamination of the crops. Industrial operations may pollute the air, land and water with these substances. Also, landfills with substantial content of these products may leach the compounds into the local drinking water. Unfortunately, employees working with these contaminants may have the highest risk.

On July 15, 2020, the Environmental Protection Agency published new water treatment and containment information about 4 additional types of PFAS compounds. The Drinking Water Treatability Database now shows chemical properties of 26 PFO and PFOA contaminants and possible treatments for local health departments.

There are steps you can take to reduce your risk. Find out from your water source whether testing for these is done regularly. Use organic/natural cleaning supplies, since other types may contain these contaminants. Investigate where foods are packaged, since recent restrictions in the United States may not be implemented where the food is packaged.   Determine whether there are any chemical processing plants or landfills in your area, and, if so, question local authorities about water sources/treatment. Lastly, try to stay informed about studies of these compounds and their health effects. [8] I do not think the expression, "What you don't know won't hurt you!" applies for these substances! Does this inspire you to action? If so, do you want to change any products you use?

Noise Pollution

9.   Have you tried, like me, to sit on a deck or patio to read, but have been inundated by the noise of power tools? Likewise, have you ever sat on the beach for peace and quiet, but had the annoyance of watercraft motors? Maybe this is why I like sailboats best!   While these limited noise experiences are disrupting, extended exposures have the greatest effect. People who work in high, steady noise environments have the most pronounced effects: hypertension, hearing loss, cardiovascular dysfunctions, psychological dysfunctions. Also, over 12% of children between the ages of 6 and 19 who regularly listen to devices at high volume had impaired hearing in one or both ears. Do you know young people who regularly listen to loud music? Do you have any influence as parents or grandparents to change this habit? [9]

The sense of hearing of whales and dolphins helps their orientation and communication. So, noise pollution from oil rigs, boats, ships, and navy vessels' sonar affects feeding habits, reproductive health, migratory patterns. Sonar has been found to cause decompression sickness in whales , which could lead to hemorrhage or death. Plus, because hearing affects location, these sea creatures have been stranded. In the United States, ship sonar is critical for defense, so coordination between scientists and military personnel is necessary for appropriate modifications [10]

Did God envision these artificial noises competing with the noise of marine animals? Do you think ocean oil drilling should be limited for the good of sea creatures?

Acid Rain

10. Isn't acid rain long gone in the US?   Actually, all that is long gone is its presence in news stories. So, maybe you say, "What is acid rain?"   Those same nasty chemicals emitted from burning the fossil fuels, sulfur dioxide and nitrogen oxides, combine with water vapor in our atmosphere. Then, the water vapor falls as acid rain on the soil, where it can leach toxic aluminum from the soil. That aluminum-laden water flows into lakes and streams, and is absorbed into root systems.

Lakes and streams which are fed by acid rain have high levels of toxic aluminum and become more acidic. Aquatic life and trees can be harmed or killed by acid rain. Also, the acidic clouds harm trees by stripping nutrients from their leaves or needles, while simultaneously the aluminum in the soil reduces water intake.   Lastly, the paint and surfaces of man-made structures like buildings, cars and statues are damaged by the acid rain. [11]

Fortunately, in the United States through the Acid Rain Program which is part of the Clean Air Act, sulfur dioxide and nitrogen oxides emissions from power plants have been greatly reduced. Annual emissions of sulfur dioxide have been decreased by 93% since 1990, while that of nitrogen oxides has been decreased by 86%. Even with this progress, concern remains about nitric levels from fertilizers and livestock feed. [12]   Do you think further regulations should be set about these pollutants?

11.   While North America has learned how to control acid rain, it is currently (in 2020) an increasing concern in Asia.

China's sulfur dioxide emissions have fallen 75% since 2007. However, India's sulfur dioxide emissions have increased by half, in other words, 1.5 times as much as in 2007. India's nitrous oxide emissions have increased by 1.42% between 1993 and 2012. [13] [14]   Since we live in a worldwide atmosphere, should developed nations have influence on the policies of developing countries?

<u>Conclude and Respond</u>

At the beginning of this lesson we considered Proverbs 25:26 (ESV):

> Like a muddied spring or a polluted fountain is a righteous man who gives way before the wicked.

Here I pose the question again: Does a "muddied spring" or "polluted fountain" imply sin? Do you believe that man is responsible for much of the pollution described in this lesson?   If so, what can we do?

Personally, I am researching some products in my home to determine if they contain PFOs or PFOAs. If possible I will replace these. I am eager to learn more about my local water supply, as far as how frequently the water is tested and what chemicals are used for treatment. I confess that I do not know where our water supply originates.

Consider this week whether any of your practices add to the pollution on our earth. Pray that God would guide leaders in setting regulations for pollution in our nation.

Lesson 12 – Action Steps
- Support organizations worldwide which help with water supply, such as "Splash," "Water.org," "Blood:Water." Search online for your choice of organization.
- Decrease personal output of Nitrous Oxide by driving less or driving electric.
- Reduce forest fires exacerbated by drought conditions by reducing global warming (Eat less beef, use manual-powered tools, drive less or use electric vehicle, plant trees.).

[1] "Pollution Impacts," Prepared by World Wildlife, accessed August 2020,   https://www.worldwildlife.org/threats/pollution

[2] "Air Pollution and Health," Prepared by United Nations Economic Commission for Europe, accessed August 2020, https://www.unece.org/environmental-policy/conventions/envlrtapwelcome/cross-sectoral-linkages/air-pollution-and-health.html

[3] "Air Pollution:How We Are Changing the Air," Prepared by University Corporation for Atmospheric Research, Center for Science Education, 2020, https://scied.ucar.edu/learning-zone/air-quality/air-pollution

[4] "Power Plant Emission Trends," Prepared by Environmental Protection Agency, 2020, https://www.epa.gov/airmarkets/power-plant-emission-trends

[5] Sanjay Kumar, "India Becomes World's Largest Emitter of Sulfur Dioxide," ChemistryWorld.com, September 3, 2019, https://www.chemistryworld.com/news/india-becomes-worlds-largest-emitter-of-sulfur-dioxide/3010917.article)

[6] "Tackling global water pollution," prepared by the United Nations Environment Assembly, accessed September 2020, https://www.unenvironment.org/explore-topics/water/what-we-do/tackling-global-water-pollution)

[7] "What Are PFOAs And PFOs And How Dangerous Are They?," prepared by The Environmental Pollution Centers, February 21, 2018, https://www.environmentalpollutioncenters.org/news/what-are-pfoa-and-pfos-and-how-dangerous-are-they/

[8] "What Are PFOAs And PFOs," prepared by The Environmental Pollution Centers,

[9] "What Is Noise Pollution?" prepared by The Environmental Pollution Center, 2017, https://www.environmentalpollutioncenters.org/noise-pollution/#:~:text=Noise%20pollution%20is%20generally%20defined,or%20consistent%20the%20exposure%20is.

[10] Wikipedia, s.v. "Marine Mammals and Sonar," accessed March 25, 2020, https://en.wikipedia.org/wiki/Marine_mammals_and_sonar#Scientific_attention

[11] "Why is Acid Rain Harmful?," Prepared by the United States Environmental Protection Agency, https://www3.epa.gov/acidrain/education/site_students/whyharmful.html#:~:text=Acid%20Rain%20Harms%20Forests&text=Acid%20rain%20that%20seeps%20into,trees%20to%20take%20up%20water.

[12] Lesley Evans Ogden, "The Bittersweet Story of How We Stopped Acid Rain," BBC.com, August 7, 2019, https://www.bbc.com/future/article/20190823-can-lessons-from-acid-rain-help-stop-climate-change

[13] Christina Nunez, "Acid Rain Explained," National Geographic, February 28, 2019, https://www.nationalgeographic.com/environment/global-warming/acid-rain/

[14] "India - Nitrous Oxide Emissions," Prepared by Knoema.com, accessed July 2020, https://knoema.com/atlas/India/topics/Environment/Emissions/Nitrous-oxide-emissions#:~:text=In%202012%2C%20nitrous%20oxide%20emissions,average%20annual%20rate%20of%201.42%25.

Lesson 13: God's Vision of the Earth on the Sixth Day: Man and Energy - Part 1

When I was a child we had one TV in our house. So between the eight of us in the house we needed to agree with the viewing choice, or not watch. Perhaps that is why we spent so much time playing outside and playing board games. Personal computers and cell phones did not exist. Dishwashers were living, breathing people who required food, not electricity. Hours of leaf raking were rewarded with play time in the pile of leaves. Despite summer temperatures reaching the 80s and 90s, we had no air conditioning.   Life certainly required less electrical power back then. I wonder what our monthly electric bill was!

In everyday life today we use quite a lot of power. Here are a few of our "requirements:" multiple TVs, dishwashers, cell phones, gas grills, leaf blowers and computers for social media and online shopping. Add to this the power we use at our jobs, schools, church and stores. Stores now take inventories through bar codes and an electricity-powered system. Churches often use electric guitars, keyboards and microphones to lead attendees who view the words on the TV screen. Office files now require electricity to generate and store. In fact, clouds even require electricity now!

This lesson begins with a look at God's design for "power" during Adam and Eve's time. Since Adam and Eve's time, not much changed in man's energy needs until the start of the Industrial Revolution in the 1800s. The first energy source used in the early 1800s was coal, followed by crude oil in the 1860s and natural gas in the 1890s. [1] Considering that these three fossil fuels are all derived from deep within the earth, we could say God created the foundations of our power supply.

1. When God created the earth there was no reason to need "power," other than manual power. Adam and Eve's needs - heat, cooking, light - were not much different from future man's needs. They did not need to drive to work, or to the grocery store, or to buy clothes. We could guess that they built their own shelter, grew and cooked their own food, made their own clothes, then taught their children how to do these tasks.   We find in Genesis 1:29 God's direction for food:

    Then God said, "I give you every seed-bearing plant on the face of the whole earth and every tree that has fruit with seed in it. They will be yours for food."

Describe how you picture life for Adam and Eve: how did they gather food, how did they cook, did they use dishes or tools, etc.

2. Later God directs man to tend the Garden of Eden. Read Genesis 2:15 and Genesis 3:17-19. What image do the phrases "painful toil" and "sweat from your brow" bring to mind?

God designed humans so that they can THINK about such tasks, then determine the best action. Adam and Eve certainly learned how to care for the garden in a manner that would enable them to feed themselves and their family. Do you care for a garden? Were you taught how to do this? By whom?

3.   In the years since Adam and Eve, man has invented many tools, techniques, fertilizers and seed varieties to produce a successful garden. What tools do you use? Is your garden just sufficient for your family's needs, or do you share the produce with others?

4.   Read these verses which refer to man's clothing:
      Genesis 3:7

      Genesis 3:21

      Proverbs 27:26

      Matt 25:36

      Proverbs 31:13

From these verses, what do you think is God's design for our clothing?

5.   What kind of labor is required to produce our clothing today? Think of all of the phases of power needed to produce one piece of clothing, starting with the crop of cotton, birth of a lamb or drilling of petroleum for polyester fabric. Consider also the power required to get the clothing into your closet, then to clean and iron it repeatedly.
A recent study compares the environmental impact (Carbon dioxide emissions and freshwater use) for these garments: T-shirt, jeans, dress, hospital uniform and jacket. [2] In terms of the carbon footprint for the service life of the garment, the jacket was the worst.   Logically, the jacket likely requires more materials and probably more complex construction which translates into a higher carbon footprint over its lifetime.   In terms of "per garment use," the carbon footprint was greatest for the dress.   A dress is a less versatile part of a wardrobe, and thus, the cost is higher per use.   If we want to reduce our environmental impact with our clothing, what should be our approach? (Ex. "The case for buying and wearing fewer dresses.") Do you think most US citizens buy more clothing than they need? Do you think that if they knew the environmental impact of clothing they would buy less and/or choose more carefully?

6.   The following bible verses refer to some of the skills man developed. Read these, then make a list of these skills.

        Exodus 35:30-35

        2 Chronicles 2:18

        Proverbs 24:27

How do you envision humans developing all of these skills? What role did God's innate gifting of each man play compared to man's ingenuity?

7.   Here are a few verses concerning God's direction about work:

        Leviticus 23:3

        Colossians 3:23

        Proverbs 14:23

        Genesis 30:28

How close to God's design for work is our work performance today?

How do you think humans can continually improve their abilities/skills/techniques?   How do you improve in your work?

8.   My husband and I are often side by side attempting to accomplish home projects. These may be as small as fixing the wire connection in an outlet, or as large as building a deck. I always have the hand screw drivers ready, while he holds the power screwdriver. My choice is about controlling the power in my hand, since the power tool seems to have a mind of its own. He is naturally after a fast

and tighter finish. In our projects I always have the ulterior motive of "helping the environment by using a hand tool rather than using electricity."

Which type of tool do you prefer?   Check the boxes as to your preference:

Task	Use power tool	Use manual tool
Wash dishes		
Wash the car		
Exercise		
Brush teeth		
Insert screws		
Chop vegetables		
Sweep the porch		
Open cans		
Trim bushes		

The bible promises in Isaiah 40:29:

He gives strength to the weary and increases the power of the weak.

This promise would seem to tell us that we could do some tasks with our own power. Why do you choose to use a power tool rather than do the task by hand? If you have children, have you taught them to do such tasks manually or with power tools?

9.   In Genesis' account of creation, there is no mention of transportation for everyday life, including to one's workplace. In Genesis 1:26 God gives man dominion over the livestock and wild animals. So, somewhere along the way man determined which animals could transport him. In later books of the Old Testament there is talk about many people building the temple. Obviously those workers needed to get to the temple to work, so perhaps they walked and/or rode on animals. How do you believe people traveled in bible times?

In the 21st century there are numerous ways to go from one place to another. As God looks at us today moving all around, what could He be thinking? Does He approve of all of man's movement?

Fuel in the Bible

10.   For ten years my husband, our kids and I lived in a house with electric heat and a wood-burning stove. At that time electricity was thought to be the most expensive way to heat a building, so the stove allowed us some relief. The kids were safe with the wooden fence we built around it, but we all probably have some carbon particle "souvenirs" in our lungs.   Years later I discovered that the stove was not the best environmental choice.

Through the Old Testament there is mention of using wood for heating and cooking. Read Isaiah 44:14-15.

Also in the Old Testament there are very specific directions for fuel, in very unique situations:
Ezekiel 39:9-10

Ezekiel 4:12-13

In each of these, decide what God's purpose was in giving these directions.

11.   In both the Old and New Testaments, olive oil is used for fuel for lamps. Read these verses to determine what God says about olive oil.

Exodus 27:20

Matthew 25:3-4

Another type of oil explicitly mentioned in the Old Testament is the oil of myrrh, to be used by Esther. Read Esther 2:12.

12.   Have you used a wood burning stove for heat or for cooking? In many areas of the world, wood is the primary fuel for heating and cooking. This persists because wood is readily available and often free. The positive aspects of this are: (a) Is renewable if forest is properly managed; (b) Could improve forest health and reduce fires; (c) Emits fewer pollutants than coal and oil if the stove is properly engineered. Wood stoves and fireplaces, especially older models, may be only 50% efficient. What could be done to help people around the world improve their use of wood fuel?

13.   Unfortunately, burning wood for heat and/or cooking has several negative effects. The tar, soot and chemicals emitted subject people in the area to respiratory health issues. The emissions of the greenhouse gases of methane and carbon dioxide, possibly as much as from burning coal, contribute to global warming. Cutting down trees not only releases carbon into the atmosphere, but

removes the carbon sink capability of a grown tree. Besides that, cutting down trees removes the cooling effect that trees have on outdoor areas and on homes.   Some Americans also like to "clear their property" to limit fall leaf cleanup and have more usable land. However, trees shade the home and yard space, saving on air conditioning bills and the need for awnings and patio cover. Do you have trees in your yard?

14.   Have you ever sat around a fire pit? In areas of the United States this, or a bonfire, are common social activities. While some respiratory risks are not as potent for outdoor fires, other negative aspects of wood burning mentioned above are present. People may believe the effect is minimal and, thus, continue this practice. How do you feel about it?

Crude Oil - One of my earliest memories about fuel was seeing my father pour gasoline from the gas can into the lawn mower. I was not clear on how the gas made the mower work. Plus, I never sought to understand how the gasoline made my parents' car move as I drove it as a teenager. Gasoline-powered vehicles have greatly influenced the advancement of society. People and goods can readily be transported not only for the necessities of life, but for the pursuit of leisure activities.

1.   Check which of the following transportation purposes you use. Next make some estimate for each as a percentage of your total travel.

Transportation Need	Check if you use	Estimate what percentage of your total transportation %
My car to work		
My car for shopping		
My car for leisure activities (friends, family, church, travel, entertainment)		
Public transit for work		
Public transit for shopping		
Public transit for leisure activities (friends, family, church, travel, entertainment)		
Air travel for work		
Air travel for leisure activities		

Of these, all likely use gasoline, except if you have a hybrid or electric vehicle. Also, some trains in the US are now powered by electricity. In working through the next sections you will learn about the relative environmental cost for each kind of fuel.

2.   You have probably seen oil wells, in pictures or in person. The idea is just like a well for water: drill down to the level where that resource flows, then pump it up for our use. Regardless of whether you believe God's creation happened in seven days, or over billions of years demarcated in the bible as "days," God "designed" the potential for crude oil formation. Isaiah 51: 16b (NIV) says:

I who set the heavens in place, who laid the foundations of the earth.

Oil's category, "fossil fuel," explains its origin: dead marine organisms such as algae are buried under sedimentary layers of rock, which are subject to high heat and high pressure over millions of years. Extracting the crude oil (as well as gas and coal) causes the release of carbon dioxide and methane.   Add to that the carbon dioxide emissions released when it is burned.   Since most of these fuels are buried in the earth, and require some amount of ingenuity to find, I wonder whether God wanted man to find them.   What do you think? If you believe God wanted humans to use fossil fuels, then what do you think God wanted us to do about the harmful effects?

3.   Gasoline-powered vehicles (car, bus, train, or airplane with jet fuel) use internal combustion. Very simply, this means the fuel burns when it mixes with air, releasing gases. These gases push the piston, which then rotates the crankshaft to stimulate the powertrain, which moves the car.   By-products of this process come out of the exhaust pipe and are commonly called, "emissions." The air-polluting emissions include carbon monoxide, carbon dioxide, nitrous oxide, non-methane organic gases (NMOG), formaldehyde and particulate matter (PM). Nitrous oxide and hydrocarbons combine to form ground-level ozone, which causes respiratory problems. [3]   Did you realize that all of these are coming out of your car?

Gasoline is one of many crude oil/petroleum products. Others you may use are: plastic containers, plastic packaging, polyester fabrics, fabrics with spandex or lycra, soap, detergents, heating oil, asphalt, bicycle tires, basketballs, nail polish, tape, paint, etc. Many of these products have been created or improved upon for the benefit of humans, to make our lives easier (and make our clothes fit better!). Talk about one or more of these items and its benefit to you in your life.

4.   Oil spills are another harmful effect of crude oil drilling. I was driving my own car at the time of the Exxon Valdez spill in 1989. This prompted me from that day forward to avoid buying Exxon gas. What seemed to be a needless accident of a ship running aground in Prince William Sound caused enduring harm to many species. It took 25 years to recover the loss of several thousand sea otters,

likely due to exposure to lingering oil. Similar effects were felt by more than 20 other near shore species. [4]

    The 2010 Deepwater Horizon Spill in the Gulf of Mexico holds the distinction of being the largest marine oil spill.   The rig exploded on April 20, then sank two days later. Up to 60,000 barrels of oil was released DAILY for months as efforts were made to stop the flow. The final court-reported total was 3.19 million barrels. A layer of oil several inches thick coated the seafloor in September, 2010. Equally alarming was the presence of microscopic oil droplets in subsurface plumes, covering about 1300 miles of the Gulf Coast. Wildlife devastation included 800,000 birds and 65,000 turtles.[5]

    Unfortunately, there are smaller spills and leakages happening all over the world . Think of it as an alien substance being added to an otherwise balanced environment, such as adding 2 Tablespoons of salt rather than sugar to your recipe. Just as that little accident changes your cookies, even a small oil leak or spill can affect the soil, ground water and air in the area.   What could be done to prevent such leaks and spills?   Do you think the company should be held responsible?

Oil Sands - In the world's quest for more power, nations have tapped into "oils sands" as an oil resource. This requires a mining process which extracts the valuable bitumen, a thick type of oil, from immense ground-level sandy pits. To be transported through pipelines for processing, bitumen generally is diluted with crude oil and chemicals. As with any mining operation, the undesirable remains, called "tailings," need to be dealt with. The water and undesirables are fed into tailing ponds, contained with a dam. It doesn't take much imagination to picture the problems with this: These ponds often contain dangerous levels of arsenic, mercury or acid, which may harm wildlife and local water supplies. Plus, there has been an average of one such dam collapse per year. In addition, the loss of the forested land that has been cleared for this process simply adds more carbon to the atmosphere. Reclamation of the land could take decades. [6]

1. How would you feel having an oil sands operation in your area?   What aspect(s) would you fear?

Natural Gas - Still to this day I am fearful about pilot lights and gas lines. As a child it seemed to be a very real concern of my parents that the pilot light on our water heater, or the pilot lights on the stove would go out. Back then this concern conjured up the image of a family suffering a horrible death by a gas explosion in their house. The idea was confirmed back then when my Great Aunt died in a gas explosion in her house only a few blocks from our house. I realize gas lines are much improved now, as are the many uses of gas in our lives.

1. It is not readily evident how much natural gas we use in our lives. Not only is it used to heat buildings and cook our food, it is also used to generate electricity. In the USA industry and electricity production comprise most of the gas use, while residential and commercial uses are also substantial. I was surprised to learn that much of the industrial use is for production of chemicals and fertilizer.

Natural gas is formed from fossils of marine organisms trapped in layers of rock far underground. The heat and pressure there break down the carbon bonds in the fossils over millions of years to produce thermogenic methane, or natural gas. [7]   In some places this gas collects in a reservoir next to impermeable rock. These reservoirs are easily "tapped" using drilling to release it, then gas pipes to transport it. The part that has not collected in neat, accessible reservoirs is primarily tapped by "fracking." (See "Fracking" section below for more detail.)

Although there is little mention in the bible about natural gas, King David does speak about other natural resources tapped for use in building the temple. Read 1 Chronicles 29:1-5. Name some of the resources mentioned. For what purpose will these resources be used?   In light of this passage, what use of our natural resources would please God most? What do you imagine God thinks about our use of fossil fuels?

2.   As with all natural resources, the natural gas will eventually be depleted. It is not renewable. What fuel will our grandchildren use if natural gas is no longer available?

3.   As with oil use, tapping and burning natural gas affects our environment. In the process of bringing natural gas to the surface, the much more potent greenhouse gas of methane is leaked. Methane has 86 times the atmospheric impact of carbon dioxide over 20 years. The technology to reduce leakage exists, but requires more investment. How do you think interest in such investment is generated?   Do you believe the government should use tax dollars for such purposes?

4.   After extraction, using the gas to generate electricity yields air pollution and greenhouse gases. The air pollutants generated are carbon dioxide, nitrous oxide, sulfuric acid, ozone and particulates. The good side of natural gas is that burning it for electricity production can be much better than burning coal. Up to 60 % less carbon dioxide is released, as well as less of the other pollutants. Nonetheless, the heat trapping effect of these emissions is still significant, and is even greater if methane leaks are not well controlled. In addition, the pollutants can cause respiratory illnesses, heart disease and cancer. [8]

If you were told that the electricity production from the natural gas power plant in your town has caused cancer in some residents, what would you do?

Coal Power - When I was very young we lived in a house that had a "coal bin," which was actually a small room in the basement next to the furnace. I recall seeing my father shovel coal from there into the furnace each night so we would sleep well. This basement room had a high window, which was designed as a coal chute. Periodically we would get deliveries from a dump truck. This was certainly much more exciting for us than the gas furnace my father eventually installed. What type of heat have you had in homes where you have lived?

1. Here we are with another of God's amazing designs in nature: Coal begins its life as plants. All plants store the sun's energy through the process of photosynthesis. (Ring a bell from elementary school?) Many millions of years ago, plant material was buried under silt, sediments and rock.   The energy stored in the plants was trapped, then subjected to intense pressure and heat, forming peat and eventually coal. Underground mining operations extract the coal, releasing the greenhouse gases, carbon dioxide and methane. Unfortunately, miners are not only subject to black lung disease, but also mining accidents and collapse. Have you ever known a coal miner?   Think about doing this type of work.   Would you ever work in a coal mine?

Fracking - Even though I recall hearing the term "fracking," it did not make an impression on me until I heard about the earthquakes in Oklahoma. Most news stories give little detail on the process, or the advantages and disadvantages of this fossil fuel extraction process. So, I will explain…

1. In recent years the USA has become a leader in fuel production through the use of the extraction method of hydraulic fracturing, or fracking. The first commercial fracking well was installed in 1947.   In areas where simple drilling techniques would not be beneficial, resources can be tapped by fracking. Remember right angles? Fracking starts by drilling vertically, or straight down. When this hole meets the horizontal shale level, the drilling makes a right angle turn into the area where the desired fossil fuel is found in small pockets. Next, fluid composed of water, chemicals and sand/ceramic particles is forced down into the well at extremely high pressure. The horizontal target shale rock absorbs the fluid to capacity, then "fractures" leaving sand and ceramic particles to hold the pathways open.

The company then extracts the resource from the opened veins, and disposes of the fluid. Because this fluid may contain pollutants and toxic chemicals, storage and disposal of it is a concern. Earthworks website says, "The oil and gas industry is the only industry in America that is allowed by EPA to inject known hazardous materials — unchecked — directly into or adjacent to underground drinking water supplies." [9] Do you think the government should regulate what chemicals are included in the fracking fluid?   Do you think there should be regulation and monitoring of the disposal of these fluids?

2. Crude oil and natural gas deposits are tapped with the fracking wells. On the positive side, this means less carbon-emitting coal is being used for electricity production, up to 50% less. The benefits are: less air pollution than coal use; more energy self-sufficiency; lower energy cost. How important do you think it is that the United States produce its own energy?

The negative aspects of fracking are: (a) leakage of the powerful greenhouse gas, methane, for which there is no regulation; (b) drinking water contamination from methane leakage and fluid disposal; (c) limited use of well, with high production in first year, and tapering to only 10% production in fifth year; (d) increased number/intensity of earthquakes in region; and (e) issues related to the need for trucking great amounts of water: deplete fresh water supplies, impact aquatic habitat, localized air pollution, road repair issues.   Knowing the disadvantages of fracking, do you think the benefit of increasing our own energy production outweighs the concerns?

Nuclear Energy - The two types of nuclear energy, fission and fusion, are covered in Lesson 7 since fusion models the sun's production of energy.

Renewable energy production is covered in the next lesson, Lesson 14. All types of energy production are included in the summary chart at the end of Lesson 14.

<u>**Conclude and Respond**</u>

Life in Adam and Eve's time differed profoundly from life today. Because of this, the fuel used in the bible, wood and olive oil, became insufficient. Man's ingenuity enabled him to develop numerous other power sources, starting with resources which God included in His design of the earth. There has almost always been a choice between a powered option and a self-powered option: hand sew our clothing, or factory-produced clothing; walk to the store or drive to the store; watch television or read a book.   Unfortunately, many of the powered options have detrimental effects on our environment.

As you consume power this week, use what you have learned here to picture what is happening to our environment.   If you make a self-powered choice, picture the good result. Pray that God will guide you to good choices. Pray that He will guide you about other actions you can take to protect the environment.

<u>**Lesson 13 – Action Steps**</u>

- Buy "vintage" second-hand clothing. Donate used clothes to second-hand shops.
- Focus on purchase of frequent-use, adaptable clothing, limiting purchases of dresses which have high environmental cost.
- Use "manual" tools whenever possible, in lieu of "power" tools.
- Limit use of fire pits and wood-burning stoves for their pollution and fossil-fuel-use impacts.
- Purchase/use electric appliances which can tap renewable resources, as preferred to gas-powered which contribute to methane release.
- Write to lawmakers to ask for further regulation of chemicals used in fracking.

---

[1] Hannah Ritchie and Max Roser, "Fossil Fuels," OurWorldinData.org, accessed August 2020, https://ourworldindata.org/fossil-fuels

[2] Roos, Sandin, Zamani and Peters, "REPORT: Environmental Assessment of Swedish Fashion Consumption," MistraFutureFashion.com, June 15, 2015, http://mistrafuturefashion.com/wp-content/uploads/2015/06/Environmental-assessment-of-Swedish-fashion-consumption-LCA.pdf

[3] Jenny Green, "Effects of Car Pollutants on the Environment," Sciencing.com, March 13, 2018, https://sciencing.com/effects-car-pollutants-environment-23581.html

[4] "25 Years After the Exxon Valdez, Sea Otter Population at Pre-Spill Levels," Prepared by US Geological Survey, February 28, 2014, https://www.usgs.gov/news/25-years-after-exxon-valdez-sea-otter-population-pre-spill-levels

[5] Richard Pallardy, "Deepwater Horizon Oil Spill," Britannica.com, April 13, 2020, https://www.britannica.com/event/Deepwater-Horizon-oil-spill

[6] Wikipedia, s.v. "Tailings - Environmental Considerations and Case Studies," accessed August 2020, https://en.wikipedia.org/wiki/Tailings#Environmental_considerations_and_case_studies)

[7] "How Do You Gather and Harvest Natural Gas?" Prepared by KB Delta Compressor Valve Parts, KBDelta.com, accessed July 2020, https://kbdelta.com/blog/gather-harvest-natural-gas.html#:~:text=The%20easiest%20way%20to%20access,are%20referred%20to%20as%20wells.

[8] "Environmental Impacts of Natural Gas," Prepared by the Union of Concerned Scientists, June 19, 2014, https://www.ucsusa.org/resources/environmental-impacts-natural-gas#:~:text=Air%20pollution,sulfur%2C%20mercury%2C%20and%20particulates.&text=Exposure%20to%20elevated%20levels%20of,%2C%20and%20cancer%20%5B11%5D.

[9] "The Halliburton Loophole," Prepared by Earthworks.org, accessed June 2020, tps://earthworks.org/issues/inadequate_regulation_of_hydraulic_fracturing/

Lesson 14: God's Vision of the Earth on the Sixth Day: Man and Energy - Part 2

I first became interested in sailboats at my childhood summer camp in southern Illinois, where a four hour sailing lesson was one of the various outdoor activities that filled the week. Ten years later, while visiting Martha's Vineyard with friends, I believed, after only that summer camp lesson, that I was prepared to rent a sailboat. There I was "prepared" enough to know that when we could not catch any wind, we had to jump ship and swim the boat in. Zoom ahead twenty years to my next attempt on our family vacation. At least this time I recognized the need for training. After two hours of training, I convinced the family I could skipper them on a two hour excursion.   Did they tell us in training that the wind changes, so that what works one day may not work the next? My poor daughter and her friend nearly fell into the bay when my son and I had to tack the sail a few times. Fortunately, we all lived to tell about it.

From these experiences I have seen the power of wind to move and control a 1000-pound sailboat. It gives me appreciation for wind power. Wind, by God's design, is freely available all around the earth, and, thus, is considered a renewable resource. Renewable means that the supply will never be exhausted, such as with fossil fuels. This lesson focuses on renewable energy: wind, hydroelectric, geothermal. Solar, which is also renewable, is covered in Lesson 7. The chart at the end of this lesson is my summary of the types of power included in this book.

1. God's control of the wind appears several times in the bible. Read these two selections and make note of God's role:

    <u>Psalm 78:26</u>

    <u>Psalm 107:25</u>

2. The bible also attributes another power source, water, to God's design for the earth. Read Psalm 65:9 (ESV):

    > You visit the earth and water it; you greatly enrich it; the river of God is full of water; you provide their grain, for so you have prepared it.

So, for both of these types God provided the resource and man figured out how to use it for his needs.

Hydroelectric Power

3.   Have you ever been in flood waters? Have you ever stood at the edge of the ocean, feeling the pull of the waves? Or, perhaps you have gone white water rafting, feeling the force of the flowing water, especially if you fall overboard! It is not difficult to understand the power of the flow of water.

Read Judges 5:21:
> The river Kishon swept them away, the age-old river, the river Kishon. March on, my soul; be strong!

In the early days of the New Testament the Greeks harnessed water power by using water wheels to grind grain. Such methods were used for mechanical power for many years after this. Ultimately, to be the most useful, this mechanical power needed to be converted to electrical power. The breakthrough came with Michael Faraday's invention of the first electric generator in 1831. This enabled the operation of the first hydroelectric power plant in Wisconsin in 1882, followed by 200 more in the USA by 1890. [1]

How does it work? First a dam is constructed to collect the river's water. Next, regulated amounts of water fall within the dam to rotate the blades of a turbine. This, in turn, spins a generator. The generator converts the kinetic energy of motion into electrical energy for our use.   The obvious benefit is a free, renewable resource with little greenhouse gas emissions. While the initial construction could create emissions, plus would be costly, ongoing operations are at minimal cost. Some environmental impact may occur from change of the landscape and water flow, plus sometimes methane is released from the reservoir. This changed landscape could also disrupt populations. How do you balance the choice of a new power source such as a hydroelectric dam with the disruption of local residents?

4.   Imagine being a farmer in an area which seems to have frequent droughts. The government wants to build a hydroelectric dam to generate electricity for your farm and include a reservoir for supplying irrigation water. Your cousins, who are farmers fifty miles downstream, are protesting because their water supply will be diminished. What do you think is the correct solution? Can this situation be handled in a fair manner?

Nile River Dams

5.   The Nile River in Africa is by God's design the longest river in the world. It is no surprise that humans have had trouble with God's gift of this river: it is shared by three countries. The first dam, the Aswan Low Dam was built from 1898 to 1902. In 1960 the Aswan High Dam was constructed, based on the 1959 resource sharing agreement between Egypt and Sudan.   (There was no mention of Ethiopia's share in this agreement.)   Man's common use of dams to control flooding and to generate power was crucial for the Aswan Dams. Finally in 2020 Ethiopia has begun constructing the massive Renaissance Dam, at the loud objection of Egypt. Here are the problems which arise when man tampers with God's design:

- **Agriculture**: The Nile River's delta region, which had been a rich agricultural treasure, through irrigation and inadequate drainage now resembles a swamp. The dams cause the water table to rise, which gives rise to an accumulation of fertilizer, pesticides and harmful salts in the soil. Nutrients necessary for agriculture have to be added through artificial fertilizers. Do you add fertilizers to your garden? Do you think God's original design for soil required fertilizers?

- **Increased Disease:** Dams create reservoirs of stagnant water. Stagnant water is breeding ground for malaria-spreading mosquitoes, West Nile virus-carrying mosquitoes and the parasitic disease, schistosomiasis. In fact the prevalence of this parasitic disease went from 21% to near 100% in some Nile regions.   The Bible tells of the plague of gnats throughout Egypt in Exodus 8:16-18. Read this. What purpose did God have for gnats at that time?   Do you believe that God has a role in any of the diseases on the Nile today?

- **Fishing Industry:** While initially the Aswan High Dam provided a beneficial fishing industry for Egypt, weed growth in the reservoir eventually reduced it to minimal value. In recent years "aquaculture," consisting of fish farms for tilapia along the Nile River, has become an important industry. These farms rely on soybean feed, which is often modified for better tilapia growth. It is no surprise that tilapia farms use modified feed, since other agricultural operations commonly use fertilizers. How do you feel about eating "farmed tilapia?" Do you believe God wants humans to "farm" tilapia?

- **Mediterranean fishing:** The dams have affected fishing in the Mediterranean Sea by sending less nutrient-rich silt and sediment from the Nile to the Sea. Before the dam, nutrient-rich river outflow, or the Nile Stream, extended along the Egyptian coast, as far west as Israel, and northward to Turkey. With less of this silt and sediment reaching the Sea, the fishing industry severely suffered. In recent years the fishing industry has improved, primarily from restocking efforts.   What impacts do you think should be studied when a dam construction project is considered?

- **Erosion:** Standing at the edge of the ocean you can feel the sand moving each time the waves recede back. Flowing water has the power to move the land underneath. This is called erosion. Read what Job says about erosion in Job 14:19:
  > "...as water wears away stones and torrents wash away the **soil**, so you destroy a person's hope."

What kind of image of erosion does this verse present?

The Nile carries silt and sediment along with it as it moves, causing two problems. First, it has reduced the inhabitable land at the delta to the Mediterranean for the first time in 10,000 years. Secondly, the silt carried from the headwater of the river to each dam gets trapped in the reservoir behind the dam. Lake Nasser behind the Aswan High Dam has become smaller each year, and thus, less effective for water and hydropower needs. Given this, it would seem that a dam has limited long-term value.

- **Population Resettlement -** Most dam projects require resettlement of some population. If dam construction was going to require people to move, do you think the dam should be built?

- (Source for all of the Nile River Dams section, "Lesson 6: The Nile River - Where Does The Water Go? By Dr. Tanya Furman and Dr. Laura Guertin") [2]

- **New Ethiopian Renaissance Dam**: Construction of a massive dam up river from those in Egypt has stirred conflict between the governments, but also conservation measures by Egypt:

> The dry years will be more severe, in that they will be hotter and more frequent," said Ethan D. Coffel. "Life is going to get much harder for farmers on the Nile." Mr.el-Sisi's Egypt has made modest efforts to prepare. Officials have imposed restrictions on water-intensive crops like rice and bananas. On Fridays, clerics deliver government-dictated sermons stressing the virtues of conservation. On Judgment Day, warned one such sermon, "God will not look favorably on water wastrels. [3]

The clerics in Egypt are Muslim. Do you think these quoted words from Muslim clerics are odd? Do you agree, as this quote suggests, that God would not look favorably on water wasters?

Do you think religious leaders should speak about conservation? Should sermons include points about environmental concerns?

How do you feel about the Nile dams? What would be most important in consideration of such a project?

Windmills

6.   Let's go back to the beginning: What is wind? Very simply, wind is moving air. If all air around the earth was the same temperature and pressure, it would not move. But since the earth is covered with land and water, and mountains and valleys, the air masses heat up differently. Warm air masses rise, while cooler air stays low, causing the air to move. Along a coastline there is much air movement with the sun heating the land during the day, and the warmth rising out of the ocean at night. (Hence: the value of coastal wind farms)

Here are some bible verses which speak of God's use of the wind. Read and make note of how God used the wind in each verse:

Genesis 8:1

1 Kings 19:11

2 Samuel 22:11

Exodus 14:21

Exodus 10:13 and 19

Did God create wind so that he could show his power with it?

7.   Did you ever use a hand-held pinwheel?   These simple toys model the wind turbines used today to generate energy. The blades in both are designed to catch the wind, then use this wind power to move them. In the 6th century Persians used windmills for irrigation and for milling grain. The first windmill used in the US was created by David Halladay in 1854, which opened the path for windmills to be used for water pumping on the American frontier.

Just like with waterwheels, man needed to find a way to turn the early windmill's mechanical energy into electricity. The first electricity-generating wind turbine was invented in 1888 in Cleveland, Ohio by Charles F. Brush. Do you recall scenes of windmills turning behind a field of tulips? This is a true depiction, since the Dutch began using windmills for the generation of electricity in the late 1800s.
 Following this, the installation of turbines on rural farms in the US became the solution for power companies who did not want the expense of extensive lines. Zoom ahead to 1981 through 1986 when California led the way with numerous installations of wind farms. Europe advanced the technology and its own installations over the next decade. [4]
Wind turbines used today for power generation are complex machines compared to windmills of the 1800s. The part you see, the blades and the shaft, are connected to a rotor, gearbox, generator and controls. Spinning blades spin the rotor, which starts the gearbox and generator, ultimately sending electricity through the power lines. Blade controls help to optimize the wind, by tilting and/or turning the blades, plus powering off at excessive wind speeds. Generally offshore wind turbines are more powerful than land turbines.[5] Benefits of wind energy are: no pollution, no emissions, new jobs and renew-ability (Wind will always be here as a result of the sun warming air masses.).
 In light of several arguments against the turbines - noise-makers, bird-killers, reduction of tourism - how do you feel about their use?   Have you considered the validity of these arguments?

8.   Question (6) above presented verses showing God's evidence of HIs power in the wind. How do you think God feels about man harvesting the wind for our power needs?

Geothermal Energy

9.   Do you ever use a steamer basket to cook vegetables? If you have not, this is a basket which is designed to hold the food above the boiling water in a saucepan.   The steam rises from the boiling water to cook the vegetables, and, thus, the nutrients do not go into the water.   The energy from the steam cooks the food. Geothermal energy follows this principle: Wells access the steam and hot water found underground, then use this to drive turbines, which in turn drive electricity generators. "Geothermal" simply means "heat from the earth."

Did you know that there are steam and hot water reservoirs deep under the earth's surface? One large such reservoir is in California. This area, called "The Geysers," fuels 23 power plants. These are a wiser choice for energy-hungry California than fossil fuel power plants.

Did you ever travel to Iceland? If so did you see a hot spring there, or a volcano? Iceland taps into its hot springs and volcanoes to generate 25% of its energy. These are the benefits of geothermal energy: low carbon dioxide emission (one-sixth of that from natural gas plants); renewable, & extended use by refilling with treated wastewater; and an uninterrupted supply. Besides being costly to build, there are some disadvantages: sulfur dioxide and hydrogen sulfide emissions; limited location viability along the path of tectonic plates; and mini-tremors in areas from well-drilling. [6]

Geothermal Heat Pump

10.   Years ago when we were house hunting, one house we liked had a geothermal heat pump. I admit I knew little about it, so perhaps that influenced our decision. That house was connected to a "ground source heat pump," which enabled the house to be heated by the warmer underground in the winter, and cooled by the cooler underground in the summer. The system simply transfers heat to and from the earth. Some electricity is needed to operate the fan, compressor and pump, but otherwise it is entirely renewable. The installation price would be a drawback, plus ground space, leaving installation in a city less feasible. [7]

Do you have a geothermal heat pump, or do you know anyone who does?   If so, what is your/their assessment of it?

Energy Storage

11.   In talking to friends about the feasibility of installing solar panels, someone usually makes the point that the solar power cannot be stored. Also, I know that electricity-generating power plants aim to produce PEAK power requirements on a regular basis, in order to not have outages at those times, but consequently produce more than needed. So, I investigated the possible power storage capabilities, and, must admit, I am amazed! There happen to be several, both existing and in development, for storing generated power:

- **My favorite:** Flywheels store electricity through high speed rotations, which, when reversed, are released as inertia energy (Do you remember the balsa wood airplanes powered by the rubber band attached to the propeller? This works the same: winding up excess energy, then "letting go" of it when needed.);
- Ice is formed at the end user site, then thawed on off hours later to fuel AC systems;
- Excess wind power is sent to residential water heaters;

- Compressed air energy storage enables produced compressed air to enhance natural gas power generation;
- Excess electricity is converted and stored as carbon-free hydrogen fuel;
- Solar energy is stored in water, molten salts or other fluids, which is converted back to power when needed;
- Battery storage capacity is constantly improving as the development of electric vehicles progresses (I drive an electric car!). Some electric power plants use batteries for storage;
- (Read more if you wish at: "How Energy Storage Works," www.ucsusa.org) [8]

Now, when someone mentions, "...but the excess cannot be stored," I have answers. Are you as excited about these capabilities as I am?

Even if you do not have solar panels, an electric car, or a geothermal heat pump, you can elect a supplier for your electricity which uses alternative energy. Here is a website to begin with, showing state-specific details:

http://competitiveenergy.org/consumer-tools/state-by-state-links/#:~:text=New%20Jersey,and%20Rockland%20Electric%20utility%20territories. [9]

Have you chosen a renewable source for your energy? If so, what is your experience with this?

Bitcoin Energy Use

12.   Have you ever purchased a bitcoin? Or, perhaps a better question, have you ever heard of bitcoin? This is a virtual currency, with no physical value, but purely investment value (or loss, as your luck would have it!) Apparently quite a lot of people worldwide have purchased these. It turns out that this "phantom currency" has an environmental cost. The cost comes in the second step: the "mining" process, which offers financial rewards to users who verify a block of transactions using powerful computers. Users all over the world create and run powerful programs, all competing to be the first to reconcile transactions. So, it is easy to imagine an energy cost. However...

Are you sitting down? It is a higher cost than you can imagine. Bitcoin's yearly energy consumption is more than that of the Czech Republic's 10.6 million people. Because the bulk of this energy is used by the "miners," they will work in areas of the cheapest fuel, like China and Mongolia. It is difficult to conclude where the miners are or what their source of fuel, because they are often anonymous. Some areas, like Quebec, Canada, have offered electricity discounts to miners to boost the local economy, whereas others like China have considered banning such currencies because of their environmental impact. [10]

How do you feel about the energy consumption by Bitcoin miners? Would you consider this energy use better if it was all from renewables?   Do you believe it is proper for governments to regulate use of such currencies?

Coronavirus 2020

13. An unexpected positive outcome of the 2020 coronavirus pandemic was decreased demand for power worldwide. If people are required to stay in their homes and communities, including not visiting retail stores and restaurants, then there is much less need for transportation of people and goods. Since I am writing this during the pandemic, in September of 2020, I am wondering what happens from here.   In the fall of 2020 do people gradually start back to their old consumption patterns? By 2021, is the world back to previous levels of consumption? There are too many variables for even the experts to see the future: behavior of people to avoid transmission; the extent of distribution of protective equipment; proven effectiveness of treatments; and the successful distribution of a vaccine. I hope that some new practices, such as working remotely, can be retained for the benefit of our environment.

 In light of the lockdowns imposed during the time of the coronavirus pandemic, how have you changed your use of power?   Name ways that the lockdown has: (a) affected your family relationships; (b) affected the activities your family does regularly; (c) affected the activities and interactions of your church body; (d) affected your transportation use; and (e) affected your job functions.

Have you heard anything about the "climate crisis" during this pandemic? What life changes could be sustained for less power use, and thus less impact on the environment?

We have family members overseas, so our intended visits had to be cancelled during the pandemic. Thanks to video chats and online gaming we have been able to regularly visit and play games. I do realize that these require power, but in lieu of air travel, there are definite environmental benefits.   How have you been able to maintain relationships with family and friends in light of travel restrictions, etc.?

Fuel Summary

Type	Uses	Pros	Cons
Coal (Solid, formed from decay of land vegetation)	Electricity generation; heating and cooking on limited basis	-- Abundant	--Dangerous mining due to explosions, fires and cancer-causing dust -- high carbon emissions --releases radioactive uranium and thorium as fly ash
Crude Oil (Liquid, formed from marine organisms from sea floor)	Gasoline for transportation; plastics, coatings, fabrics, asphalt, soaps, paint	-- Variety of refining methods allow numerous uses	-- Limited supply -- Extraction emissions -- Emissions from burning -- Oil spills
Natural Gas (Gas, formed from marine organisms from sea floor)	Fuel for cooking, heating and water heating; electricity generation,	-- Fewer harmful emissions than coal and oil, if leaks are controlled	--Small volumes at large depths; limited supply --Leaks of methane, a potent greenhouse gas
Oil Sands (extracted as the heavy liquid, bitumen	Yields synthetic crude oil, refined to make asphalt, gasoline, jet fuel and value-added chemicals.	-- Extends oil resource for future demands	--Remove forrest before extraction --Waste ponds toxic to ducks and birds --Requires 3 barrels of fresh water for 1 barrel of oil --Cleanup of mines and trailings expensive --Creates wasteland, needs to be reclaimed --Causes air pollution and toxic rain
Windmills	Electricity generation	-- No pollution -- No emissions -- New jobs -- Renewable (Wind will always be here as a result of the sun warming air masses.).	-- Noise -- Kill birds (although less than pollution & habitat destruction) -- Reduction of tourism
Solar Panels	Spacecraft, electricity generation, solar devices	-- No greenhouse emissions from use -- Require little maintenance	-- Some greenhouse emissions from production -- High initial cost -- Effectiveness depends on sunlight
Wood	Heating, cooking, social gatherings, camping	--Price relatively stable --Short-term renewable life compared to fossil fuels --Using forest wastes improves forest health. By removing deadfalls from the forest, the practice can reduce forest-fire hazards. --With proper engineering, wood-burning systems emit	---Renewability depends on good forest management --Pollution from tar, soot and chemicals --Efficiency for home units may only be 50% --As "dirty" as coal from methane, particles and black carbon --Wood burning emits as

		fewer pollutants into the air than coal and oil.	much carbon dioxide as coal burning --Cutting trees releases carbon from soil and tree into atmosphere, removes carbon-absorber tree
Nuclear Fission (Uses uranium)	Electricity	-- Near zero carbon dioxide emissions, since not produced from fossil fuels -- 24-hour production -- Minimal annual maintenance periods	-- Potential for nuclear accident/leakage -- Disposal of nuclear waste -- Uranium is a non-renewable resource -- Costly
Nuclear Fusion (Mimics the sun)	Electricity	-- Uses lithium and hydrogen, both are plentiful	-- No carbon emissions -- No meltdown potential --Produces much less radioactive waste than nuclear fission
Hydroelectric power	Electricity	-- No fossil fuel, so no greenhouse emissions -- Relatively low ongoing cost -- Renewable, through rainfall	-- Costly initial investment -- Can affect land and water wildlife habitat -- Can affect local land management -- Methane could form in reservoir, adding to greenhouse emissions
Geothermal power	Electricity, or heat and cooling for buildings	-- Low carbon dioxide emission (one-sixth of that from natural gas plant) -- Renewable, & extended use by refilling with treated wastewater -- Uninterrupted supply	-- Emits sulphur dioxide and hydrogen sulphide -- Location-specific along tectonic plates -- Costly to build -- Mini-tremors in area from well-drilling
Geothermal Heat Pump	Heating and cooling for buildings; possible hot water included	-- Renewable -- No greenhouse gas emissions -- Per dollar more beneficial to power grid than solar and wind	-- Requires minimal electricity -- Expensive initial installation, recouped over several years

Conclude and Respond

So much of God's blueprint for our earth is not readily evident. This is the case with the numerous options for power. Adam did not know that he could harness geothermal resources, the heat or cold held in the ground, to heat their shelter on cold days and to cool their shelter on warm days. His wife would have been really impressed if he did. Fortunately, long after Adam and Eve explored the earth man learned how to use the not-so-evident resources for his power needs. Unfortunately, man has exponentially expanded his need for energy, with some harmful results.

Review your energy needs this week to assess if changes are possible. Also, consider the installation of alternative energy, or simply the choice of a renewable energy provider. Pray that God would direct your choices and actions.

Lesson 14 – Action Steps
- Do not buy virtual currencies such as Bitcoin.
- Many states allow energy choice; if you are able to, choose a renewable provider. Otherwise, consider installing solar panels.
- When building a new home, consider installing Geothermal heat/air conditioning, or solar panels.

[1] Robert W.Shortridge, "Some Early History of Hydroelectric Power," www.hydroreview.com, June 1988. http://www.hydroreview.com/wp-content/uploads/content/dam/hydro/Document/earlyhistoryrev2.pdf

[2] Dr. Tanya Furman and Dr. Laura Guertin, "Lesson 6: The Nile River - Where Does The Water Go?," Penn State College of Earth and Mineral Sciences, accessed July 2020, https://courseware.e-education.psu.edu/courses/earth105new/content/lesson06/04.html

[3] Declan Walsh and Somini Sengupta, "For Thousands of Years, Egypt Controlled the Nile. A New Dam Threatens That," The New York Times, February 9, 2020, ttps://www.nytimes.com/interactive/2020/02/09/world/africa/nile-river-dam.html

[4] "History: Early Wind Power," Prepared by Thirdplanetwind.com, accessed July 2020, http://www.thirdplanetwind.com/energy/history.aspx#:~:text=The%20earliest%20known%20wind%20powered,in%20his%20Connecticut%20machine%20shop.

[5] "Basics of Wind Energy," Prepared by American Wind Energy Association, accessed August 2020, https://www.awea.org/wind-101/basics-of-wind-energy

[6] Jack Unwin, "What is Geothermal Energy?," Power-technology.com, June 18, 2019, https://www.power-technology.com/features/what-is-geothermal-energy/

[7] Jay Egg, " 10 Myths About Geothermal Heating and Cooling," National Geographic, September 17, https://www.nationalgeographic.com/environment/great-energy-challenge/2013/10-myths-about-geothermal-heating-and-cooling/

[8] "How Energy Storage Works," Prepared by the Union of Concerned Scientists, www.ucsusa.org , February 19, 2015, https://www.ucsusa.org/resources/how-energy-storage-works#:~:text=Many%20hydroelectric%20power%20plants%20include,through%20turbines%20to%20generate%20electricity.

[9] "State by State Information," Prepared by American Coalition of Competitive Energy Suppliers, accessed July 2020, http://competitiveenergy.org/consumer-tools/state-by-state-links/#:~:text=New%20Jersey,and%20Rockland%20Electric%20utility%20territories.

[10] Umair Irfan, "Bitcoin is an Energy Hog. Where is all that Electricity Coming From?," Vox.com, June 18, 2019, https://www.vox.com/2019/6/18/18642645/bitcoin-energy-price-renewable-china

Lesson 15 - Part 1: God's Vision of the Earth: Seventh Day

Admit it: you like to rest sometimes! After a very busy day I am eager to sit back in a comfy chair to read a good book, or watch a favorite show. God knows that man needs rest. He never expected man to work continually day after day without rest. Compare how you feel if you have rested for an afternoon, versus how you feel if you do cleaning or yard work or any work all afternoon.

1.   God gives us an example: resting from his creation work on the seventh day. Read Genesis 2:1-3.

2.   On some days I feel very productive, perhaps "inspired."   I feel very passionate about the "work" I am doing, even if it is a hobby. At such times I hesitate to take a break, or to even go to sleep at a reasonable hour. Do you ever feel like that?

While God was creating the earth I suspect that He felt like that: very passionate about His work. The Genesis account repeats the statement, "God saw that it was good." And yet, He took a break each day, then continued working the next day. How well do you follow God's example in this? Do you get enough daily rest?

3.   Once he had completed creation in the way He envisioned it, He was pleased. Genesis 1:31 says: " God saw everything He had made, and indeed, it was very good." Then, on the seventh day, as Genesis 2:1-3 shows, God rested from all of the work He had done. At this time He was simply setting an example. Later in Exodus God commands the Israelites to keep the Sabbath holy as one of the Ten Commandments. Read Exodus 20:8-10. What are they told NOT TO DO?   What are they told TO DO?

4.   Different congregations espouse different rules about "keeping the Sabbath Day holy." The New Testament accounting of Jesus healing the crippled woman on the Sabbath has influenced some interpretations. Read Luke 13:10-17. How does Jesus justify his actions?
Some churches believe that "doing God's work" is allowed on Sunday. What does your religious institution direct about this? Do you regularly follow this direction?

5.   God was pleased with His creation. On each of the first six days, the text notes:

God saw all that he made, and it was very good. (Genesis 1:31 - NIV)

Imagine what the earth was like at the end of the sixth day. Describe this.

How does this picture of God's creation differ from what the earth looks like today? What do you imagine God thinks about the earth today?

<u>Conclude and Respond</u>
On the seventh day God modeled the importance of resting after work. Just as humans can use their brain to exercise dominion, God directed us to allow that brain and our body to rest.   Monitor yourself this week to be sure that you are resting enough and in the right manner. Pray that God would restore you and refresh you through good rest times.

<u>God's Good Earth</u> bible study book concludes with one last section: Part 2 - What Does God Want of Us At This Time? You are asked to assess your understanding and position in light of all you have read and studied.

Lesson 15 - Part 2: What Does God Want of Us At This Time?

Ever since I learned about climate change in college (many years ago!), I have tried to make good choices for the environment. I force my family to use real dishes, cloth napkins, cloth cleaning rags and kitchen towels. I went so far as to use only real dishes and cloth napkins for a ninety-person yard party we hosted.   I ignore my family's persuasion by hand-washing dishes while standing next to the dishwasher. When my little sports car was "getting up in years," I purchased an electric car. I believe this was perhaps the BEST purchase I ever made.   My actions are prompted by alarm about how our God-given environment is deteriorating, and concern for my children, future grandchildren and future great-grandchildren.

1. Knowledge of the worldwide situation is so important. Read each of these verses concerning knowledge:
    Psalm 119:66

    <u>Ecclesiastes 7:12</u>b

Some denominations include the Apocrypha section in their bible.   Other denominations do not include these books as part of the inspired bible text. One reference from this section (<u>Wisdom 9:11</u>) tells us what to do with our knowledge:

> For she knows and understands all things, and she will guide me wisely in my actions and guard me with her glory.

Do you think you now have the knowledge to guide your actions?

2.   Read Isaiah 24:4-6:

> The earth mourns and withers; the world languishes and withers; the highest people of the earth languish. The earth lies defiled under its inhabitants; for they have transgressed the laws, violated the statutes, broken the everlasting covenant. Therefore a curse devours the earth, and its inhabitants suffer for their guilt; therefore the inhabitants of the earth are scorched, and few men are left.

Where does this verse lay the blame for the earth languishing and withering? What did the people do?

Do you believe this verse could apply to any environmental degradation happening now in the 21st century? Does man's greed and adoration of idols have anything to do with the earth's condition?   If so, what should man do now?

Climate Justice

3.   Unfortunately the situation described in Isaiah 24:4-6 is reality in some parts of the world. Besides those presented throughout this book, here are a few:

- Due to an unprecedented devastating drought in Kenya in 2009, one of many stricken farmers reported cattle herds reduced from 200 to 20. Equally affected was agricultural output, causing severe food shortages. [1]
- A Ugandan woman told of the years from 2000 to 2009 vacillating from flash floods to droughts amidst erratic seasons. She admitted that she originally believed some horrendous wrongdoing of her people had wrecked God's vengeance on them. However, with her research as part of a climate conference, she now concludes that it is "the rich people in the west that are doing this to us." [2]
- After Hurricane Katrina ravaged the southern US in 2005, the Mississippi government was promised federal aid, with a requirement that 50% be used for low-income poor. However, Governor Barbour requested that this requirement be dropped. By November 2007 his government had spent 1.7 billion on mid- and upper-level income homeowners and businesses, but only $167 million for programs for low-income residents. [3]
- As of 2018 1.3 billion people worldwide still have no electricity, and 2.6 billion people still cook over open fires. [4]
- Based on current trends, if global temperatures increase by 2° C (1880 to 2050), water shortages around the world will double from 2018 levels. [5]
- Seventy percent of the food consumed worldwide is from small farms and subsistence farmers in Africa and Asia. So, environmental changes there profoundly impact world food supply. [6]

These examples illustrate how environmental degradation will primarily impact the low-income people of the world. All of these cases, and numerous others, are documented in a book by Mary Robinson, the past President of Ireland. She says:

> ... Gradually changing weather patterns and rising sea levels were slowly and steadily causing greater food shortages, pollution, and poverty, putting decades of development advances at risk. This injustice - that those who had done least cause the problem were carrying the greatest burden - made clear that to advocate for the rights of the most vulnerable to food, safe water, health, education and shelter would have no effect without paying attention to our world's changing climate. [7]

Do you agree that some of the wealthy nations of the world have had a greater impact on climate change? How do you feel about calling this "an injustice?"

After all that you have studied in this book, do you believe that climate change will need to be addressed **before** or at least **simultaneously with** other food shortage, water supply and population issues?

4.   There are a few ways to look at the changes in our environment:

a) God knew humans would have done all of this to the earth, and He allowed it to happen. So, it is His plan. We do not need to do anything differently.

b) If our earth becomes uninhabitable, this is simply the fulfillment of the prophecies in the bible. It precedes the second coming. We do not need to do anything differently.   See Revelations 21:1:
> Then I saw a new heaven and a new earth, for the first heaven and the first earth had passed away, and the sea was no more.

c) God allows humans "free choice," which has led to choices that have not benefited human life. "Human life" covers God's people worldwide, so we must seek to study other lands. God would want us to use our brains to make the whole earth more sustainable and bring it closer to the way that He designed it.

d) Man does have "free choice," but I do not believe my personal actions will have any effect.

Since you have completed this study of our environment, which of the above views do you ascribe to?

Images of Man's Impact

5.   Quite often in this book you have read that global warming has caused changes from God's design. This is an abstract concept for us, even if we think in terms of our "carbon footprint."   The problem is: no matter how fired-up I get about these concerns, many people I talk to are not alarmed, or at least not alarmed enough to change. No matter how many good arguments I name, or how logical my explanation is, most people will not be moved to act. Perhaps the environmental concerns presented in this lesson are not personal yet: there are no wildfires, hurricanes or floods near their homes, and no one they know is starving due to poor food supply.

Many people feel that their action would have little effect. To better illustrate impact and action, I summarize an excellent article:

- One gallon of gas generates 20 pounds of carbon dioxide, meaning an average of 10,000 pounds per year. This amount of gas would more than fill a tourist **hot air balloon**.
- An American's average annual carbon dioxide emissions (16 metric tons) would fill **four such balloons**.
- Consider 330 million Americans at 4 balloons each puts **1.3 billion CO2hot air balloons** in the air annually.
- These 1.3 billion hot air balloons added every year stay **in the atmosphere at least 300 years**, continually adding to those from previous years.
- **Add balloons from all other earthly inhabitant**s to these 1.3 billion annual balloons from the United States. If they were real balloons, we might never see the sun, moon or stars.
- A quarter pound beef burger generates 6 pounds of CO2emissions, ten times more than ¼ pound of tofu.
- Driving one mile in your car spews emissions equivalent to emissions from 10 miles on a commuter train.
- Source for all bullets: Tim Dickinson, "The True Cost of Carbon," by *Rolling Stone,* April 2020 [8]

Does the image of the balloons surprise you? Do you think that if more humans could picture this impact it would change their actions?

Personal Actions

6.   Perhaps you are now concerned, but do not know what to do. Or, you feel your changes will have no impact. Please do not feel like that!   Every little change each of us makes adds up. In other words, you may add one, two, or three less hot air balloons in the above illustration.

Here is a ranked list of personal actions for their benefit of reducing carbon footprint, from least to greatest [9]:

- Upgrade light bulbs (**least benefit**)
- Hang laundry to dry
- Recycle
- Wash clothes in cold water
- Vegetarian diet
- Buy green energy
- Cancel a trans-Atlantic flight
- Switch to an electric car
- Don't use a car
- Have one less kid (**greatest benefit**)

About the most effective way, **having one less child**, alarm bells go off as some think about China's Two-Child Policy and subsequent One Child Policy.   Not so fast: this article's ranking is based simply on the facts of an average human's impact on the earth as regards food, clothing, shelter, transportation, children, grandchildren, etc. The article compares this impact to that of a trans-Atlantic flight, changing a dozen light bulbs, installing solar panels, driving an electric car, etc. No environmentalist is asking a person not to have a baby. No environmentalist is asking for government legislation to limit family size. This article goes back to the "uphill battle" I described in the introduction. Each person goes through the uphill steps, then decides what he or she is willing to change.

For my husband and I, we talked about having three children before our wedding. In subsequent years we had our first, then our second child. This just seemed right for us, so we abandoned the idea of three children.   My purpose in this book is not to question any person's choice, or to even discuss an approach to making such choices. My goal is to simply present information I have found about restoring the earth as God designed it for us to thrive.

Based on this ranking of the impact of actions, do you see any personal actions that you could change?

Government Role

7.   As mentioned in several places in this book, governments make decisions about setting regulations, monitoring the standards of the law, banding with other governments and/or organizations for action, etc. In the United States our democracy allows citizens to have a voice in the government at all levels. Each of us has a responsibility to research candidates and determine whose policies best meet our concerns. Just as writing this book has been much easier in 2020 than it would have been in 2000 with the extensive internet, researching candidates is very easy through the internet. A well-informed voter seeks information from several sources to assure a well-rounded analysis. Do this, then vote according to your convictions!

8.   (Warning: This part may be too sad...)   If you continue reading in the bible, way past Genesis, to almost the end, you will find a desolate view of our earth. Read these verses to see earth's future:

2 Peter 3:10

Revelation 8:7

<u>Revelation 9:18</u>

Revelation 16:8

What do these verses tell us about the end of the earth?

The scene is not good. The question comes to mind: how much time will pass until the earth is destroyed in this manner? No one knows, as the bible tells us in Matthew 24:35-36:

> Heaven and earth will pass away, but my words will not pass away. But about that day or hour no one knows, not even the angels in heaven, nor the Son, but only the Father.

9.   (...but there is hope...)   In the meantime, I believe God would want us to do our best to keep the earth inhabitable for future generations worldwide. We can do this, with the intelligence and abilities God gave us.

Do you believe that God would want us to take care of the earth until we pass away, or until the earth passes away? Do you believe that God would want us to care for our neighbors in other lands?

Let Go – Let God

Perhaps this book should have started with this topic then, no other topics would have been needed! The reason I include it at the end is that I believe God often asks us to "do our part," while He will respond to our prayers and do his part. For example, we can pray endlessly asking God to lead us to a new job, but likely nothing will happen unless we send out applications and resumes. Thus, while responding in any way that you can to any of the challenges presented in this book, we can also seek God's guidance and spiritual help. Here are a few ways to ask for God's help in tackling climate change:

1.   **Pray** – I admit that as a child and teenager I said the words of the Our Father and Hail Mary prayers by rote with little understanding of the meaning. Probably a nun during my eight years of parochial school explained theses prayers to my class. Praying via these prayers is good if you understand the meaning. One aspect of the meaning is praise and honor for God.   This type of prayer is important, and should accompany your requests. Do you use either of these, or other prepared prayers to pray?

2. As a young adult I learned another way to pray. To do this simply act like you are talking to a friend, parent or spouse.   After praising God, then just ask God for what you need, even if it is wisdom. For example, "God, I ask that you help me to make a decision about college." Or you might say, "God, help me to find a resource for food while I am out of work." Read Philippians 4:6 (NIV):

>   Do not be anxious about anything, but in every situation, by prayer and petition, with thanksgiving, present your requests to God.

Do you pray like this?

3. **Hope in Prayer** – An important element of prayer is HOPE. When you pray you should believe that an answer will be coming. By believing you are clearing your anxiety about the issue. The topic of this section is, "Let Go and Let God."   So, be sure to hand your request over to God with the hope that He will help. The bible explains this in these verses:

>   Mark 11:24 (NIV) - Therefore I tell you, whatever you ask for in prayer, believe that you have received it, and it will be yours.

>   Romans 12:12 (NIV) - Be joyful in hope, patient in affliction, faithful in prayer.

Since our minds tend to fight us on this, how good are you about "letting go" when you pray?

4. **Answers to Prayer** - When we make a request, we expect an answer. Naturally when we pray, we expect an answer. Over the years when hearing my mother's anxious words, I would pray with her over the phone or in person. I made sure to always ask God for, "the best possible answer." With these words I was leaving the outcome to God, rather than telling him what we wanted. It was amazing how God answered: almost always with a very good outcome!   In one instance after her heart attack, we asked for "the best possible answer" regarding the extent of damage. The amazing answer was that there was *no damage*! Years later, our prayers for "the best possible outcome" for her pancreatic cancer surgery were answered with the diagnosis, "stage one, non-invasive." I started to think that she had some special connection to God, but the truth must have simply been that she was meant to be with us longer.

These bible verses speak of God's answers to prayer:

Psalm 65:2 (NIV) - You who answer prayer, to you all people will come.

>   Zechariah 10:6 (NIV) - "I will strengthen Judah and save the tribes of Joseph. I will restore them because I have compassion on them. They will be as though I had not rejected them, for I am the LORD their God and I will answer them.

What kind of answers to your prayers have you had?

5. **Prayers for our Environment** – Even though environmental concerns in biblical times were usually not the same as those we face now, such prayers and their answers are documented in the bible.   Read these verses and make note of the "environmental" answer from God:

> Psalm 65:5 (NIV) - You answer us with awesome and righteous deeds, God our Savior, the hope of all the ends of the earth and of the farthest seas.
>
> 2 Chronicles 7:14 (NIV) - If my people, who are called by my name, will humble themselves and pray and seek my face and turn from their wicked ways, then I will hear from heaven, and I will forgive their sin and will heal their land.
>
> James 5:18 (NIV) - Again he prayed, and the heavens gave rain, and the earth produced its crops.
>
> Exodus 9:29 (NIV) - Moses replied, "When I have gone out of the city, I will spread out my hands in prayer to the LORD. The thunder will stop and there will be no more hail, so you may know that the earth is the LORD's.
>
> God's "Environmental" answers:

6. So, it seems that God can change our environment. Christians could pray for God's "revival" of our earth, its restoration back to its original design in order that it will be able to sustain human life long term. This is certainly a valid prayer. How do you feel about such an approach?

7. While praying for God's help, I believe it is important to "Do Our Part," too. Throughout these lessons the "Conclude and Respond" sections often asked the reader to seek God's guidance about actions to be taken. There are several ways to do this:

- Ask God to help you establish new environmentally-helpful habits.
- Ask God to provide focus on specific areas for action.
- Ask God to lead you through action steps.
- Ask God to help you find like-minded people.
- Ask God to inspire you through good leaders.
- Ask God to inspire you through understandable reading materials.

<u>**Conclude and Respond**</u>

Perhaps you feel somewhat overwhelmed with the numerous topics presented in this study. Nevertheless, I admit that there were many other related topics which I could have covered. My hope is that you will continue to study our environmental situation. Maybe like me you will tag online articles, cut out newspaper articles, pay attention to news broadcasts, and tell friends and families about your findings. And, if like me, your enthusiasm to help the state of affairs has grown/will grow. Together we can give future generations a sustainable, beautiful earth, as God would want us to do.

<u>**Lesson 15 – Action Steps**</u>

- Act on one or more of the steps suggested in this book; the **<u>sum</u>** of our small steps will make a difference.
- Read <u>Climate Justice</u> by Mary Robinson.
- Write to lawmakers for regulation of FEMA disaster relief to assure more even distribution across economic classes.
- Always make the effort to vote, and to make an informed decision.
- Consider your "idols," such as material goods that are not necessities. Can you reduce your consumption?
- **Pray** for direction from God!

---

[1] Mary Robinson, <u>Climate Justice</u> (Berryville, VA: Berryville Graphics, Inc., 2018), p. 15.

[2] Robinson, <u>Climate Justice</u>, p. 16-17.

[3] Robinson, p. 38.

[4] Robinson, p. 8.

[5] Robinson, p. 6

[6] Robinson, p. 21.

[7] Robinson, p. 4.

[8] Tim Dickinson, "The True Cost of Carbon," by <u>Rolling Stone</u>, April 2020, https://www.rollingstone.com/culture/culture-features/how-to-reduce-carbon-emissions-971990/

[9] Seth Wynes and Kimberly A. Nicholas, "2017 Environmental Research Letters," in Tim Dickinson, "The True Cost of Carbon," <u>Rolling Stone</u>, April 2020, https://www.rollingstone.com/culture/culture-features/how-to-reduce-carbon-emissions-971990/

Author Notes

Whatsoever thy hand findeth to do, do it with thy might; for there is no work, nor device, nor knowledge, nor wisdom, in the grave, whither thou goest.   Ecclesiastes 9:10 (KJV)

With over 40 years of personal study on environmental topics, I am passionate about preserving our environment. The noted verse from Ecclesiastes reminds me to continually act on my passion. My extensive experience in teaching bible classes, leading bible studies and participating in many bible studies has shown me the value of bible study/instruction in small groups. That is exactly why I have prepared this bible study guide for an in-depth look at the earth's environment. Seeing how our planet's current condition differs from the earth which God created may cause concern or ring alarm bells. Ultimately, my hope was to open eyes to some of the impact of climate change, and to encourage action.

Yes, I did consider the environmental impact of another book, either as print or as an energy-guzzling ebook. However, I saw no other way to communicate the extent of the situation without using a book format. I anticipate that the "environmental cost" of this book will be far compensated by the resulting actions of the readers!

Personal Study

Would you like to read this book, but not as part of a study group? Do it! Reading each section is easily accomplished in the same manner you would read a non-fiction article or book. The information can be individually evaluated. All of the questions posed are for personal reflection.

Leader Notes

- Introduction: Do this with the study participants in the first session, along with "Lesson 1." There are important introductory notes to set the tone for the lessons.
- Each lesson includes several topics related to that lesson theme. Depending on the time allowed for your sessions, you may cover all topics, or skip some in order to end the session with the "Conclude and Respond" section. If you skip some, I suggest that you ask participants to read those at home, since, as you can guess, I think **all** are important!
- Lesson 15 has two parts, one which covers the Seventh Day of Rest, and the second which wraps up the entire book. This conclusion section, "**Lesson 15 - Part 2: What Does God**

Want of Us At This Time?," is quite important for analysis of your participants' understanding and response.
- This book is available in print format, or ebook format. The print book leaves some area for participant notes after the questions. If using the ebook, then it is recommended that you have the participants use notebooks, or an online app for note.
- Yes, I did consider the environmental impact of another book, either as print or as an energy-guzzling ebook. However, I saw no other way to communicate the extent of the situation without using a book format. I anticipate that the "environmental cost" of this book will be far compensated by the resulting actions of the participants!

General Notes to keep in mind….
- **NOTE**: The words "man" and "human" are always used in this book to denote BOTH man and woman.
- Bible verses: If there was only one reference verse, then the text is included. If there are multiple verses for one reference, OR multiple pertinent references, then the reader/leader is asked to look up the verses.
- In most cases I have marked the version used. However, there is **no** definitive choice for any references. I have found in my groups that hearing a few versions adds to the discussion.

Works Cited

American Academy of Allergy Asthma and Immunology. "Does Climate Change Impact Allergic Disease?"
    https://www.aaaai.org/conditions-and-treatments/library/allergy-library/climate-change

Andrews, Paul. "Who Drained Russia's Vast Aral Sea?" Wordpress.com, April 30, 2018,
    https://paulwandrews.wordpress.com/2018/04/30/who-drained-russias-vast-aral-sea/

Baker, Aryn. "Plastics Still Manage to Reach the End of the World," *Time Magazine.* April 9, 2020,
    https://time.com/5818225/microplastics-
    antartica/#:~:text=An%20estimated%208%20million%20metric,in%20the%20ocean%20by%202050.

Barnard, Anne. "Climate Change Is Killing the Cedars of Lebanon," July 18, 2018,
    https://www.nytimes.com/interactive/2018/07/18/climate/lebanon-climate-change-environment-
    cedars.html#:~:text=But%20some%20trees%20can%20survive,reserve%20has%20just%202%2C100%20tre
    es.

Becktold, Wendy. "Much Ado About Mushrooms," *Sierra Magazine,* May/June 2020

Bendix, Aria. "The US Just Banned 12 Pesticides that are Like Nicotine for Bees. Here's How Dangerous They Are,"
    Business Insider, May 30, 2019, https://www.businessinsider.com/epa-banned-pesticides-killing-bees-2019-
    5#:~:text=The%20US%20Environmental%20Protection%20Agency,to%20the%20world's%20crop%20produc
    tion

Bernstein MD, Aaron. "Climate Change and Allergies," Harvard TH Chan School of Public Health,
    https://www.hsph.harvard.edu/c-change/subtopics/climate-change-and-allergies/

Berwyn, Bob. "Avalanches Menace Colorado as Climate Change Raises the Risk," *Insideclimate News,* March 9, 2019,
    https://insideclimatenews.org/news/08032019/avalanche-climate-change-

Borunda, Alejandra. "What a 100-Degree Day in Siberia Really Means, *National Geographic,* June 23, 2020,
    https://www.nationalgeographic.com/science/2020/06/what-100-degree-day-siberia-means-climate-change/

Brennan, R, Jan, JE & Lyon, CJ. "Light, Dark, and Melatonin: Emerging Evidence for the Importance of Melatonin in
    Ocular Physiology." *Nature.* Sept. 22, 2006,
    https://www.nature.com/articles/6702597#:~:text=Melatonin%20is%20a%20hormone%2C%20which,cycles%
    2C%20thus%20regulating%20melatonin's%20secretion

Bunge, Jacob. "Roundup Ruled the Farm, Now Its Maker Has a Challenger," *The Wall Street Journal,* Jan. 6, 2020,
    https://www.wsj.com/articles/roundup-ruled-the-farm-now-its-maker-has-a-challenger-
    11578328409#:~:text=Roundup%20revolutionized%20farming%20when%2C%20combined,It%20is%20still%
    20No.&text=Many%20in%20the%20industry%20expect,weeds%20than%20most%20other%20herbicides.

Burke, Minyvonne. "Video shows koalas, other animals hurt in Australia's fires getting treated," *NBC News,* Jan.10,
    2020, https://www.nbcnews.com/news/world/video-shows-koalas-other-animals-hurt-australia-s-fires-getting-
    n1113436

Butler, Rhett A. "Deforestation in Brazil Continues Torrid Pace into 2020," Mongabay Series, Feb.9, 2020,
    https://news.mongabay.com/2020/02/deforestation-in-brazil-continues-torrid-pace-into-2020/

Calma, Justine. "What You Need to Know About the Australia Bushfires," The Verge, February 13, 2020,
    https://www.theverge.com/2020/1/3/21048891/australia-wildfires-koalas-climate-change-bushfires-deaths-
    animals-damage

Carrington, Damain. "World's Largest Nuclear Fusion Project Begins Assembly in France," *The Guardian*, July, 28,
    2020, https://www.theguardian.com/environment/2020/jul/28/worlds-largest-nuclear-fusion-project-under-
    assembly-in-france

Carrington, Damian. "Ocean temperatures hit record high as rate of heating accelerates," *The Guardian,* Jan.13, 2020,
    https://www.theguardian.com/environment/2020/jan/13/ocean-temperatures-hit-record-high-as-rate-of-
    heating-accelerates)

Chappell, Bill. "Jakarta Is Crowded And Sinking, So Indonesia Is Moving Its Capital To Borneo," National Public Radio,
    Aug. 26, 2019, https://www.npr.org/2019/08/26/754291131/indonesia-plans-to-move-capital-to-borneo-from-
    jakarta#:~:text=Asia-
    ,Jakarta%20Is%20Crowded%20And%20Sinking%2C%20So%20Indonesia,Moving%20Its%20Capital%20To
    %20Borneo&text=AFP%2FGetty%20Images-
    ,Indonesian%20President%20Joko%20Widodo%20(center)%20says%20the%20new%20capital%20city,on%

20the%20island%20of%20Borneo.&text=The%20capital's%20current%20location%20faces,the%20fact%20that%20it's%20sinking.

Chen, Jialu. "Does Using Paper Take CO2 Out of the Environment ?" *Mother Jones,* April 4, 2012,
https://www.motherjones.com/environment/2012/04/paper-carbon-dioxide-sequester/

Chow, Denise. "Three Islands Disappeared in the Past Year. Is Climate Change to Blame?" NBC News, June 9, 2019,
https://www.nbcnews.com/mach/science/three-islands-disappeared-past-year-climate-change-blame-ncna1015316

Chu, Elizabeth and Tarazano, D. Lawrence. "A Brief History of Solar Panels," *Smithsonian Magazine*, April 22, 2019,
https://www.smithsonianmag.com/sponsored/brief-history-solar-panels-180972006/

Cirino, Erica. "What Do the Birds and the Bees Have to Do With Global Food Supply?," Audubon.org, March 10, 2016,
https://www.audubon.org/news/what-do-birds-and-bees-have-do-global-food-supply

Daley, Beth. "Explainer: how the Antarctic Circumpolar Current helps keep Antarctica frozen". *The Conversation,* Nov. 15, 2018, https://theconversation.com/explainer-how-the-antarctic-circumpolar-current-helps-keep-antarctica-frozen-106164

Dasgupta, Shreya. "How Many Plant Species Are There in the World? Scientists Now Have an Answer," May 12, 2016,
https://news.mongabay.com/2016/05/many-plants-world-scientists-may-now-answer/

Davenport, Coral.   "Trump Eliminates Major Methane Rule, Even as Leaks Are Worsening," *The New York Times*,
Aug. 20, 2020, https://www.nytimes.com/2020/08/13/climate/trump-methane.html

Davis, Nicola . "Scientists Confirm Dramatic Melting of Greenland Ice Sheet," *The Guardian.* April 15, 2020,
https://www.theguardian.com/science/2020/apr/15/scientists-confirm-dramatic-melting-greenland-ice-sheet

Department of Systematic Biology, Entomology Section, National Museum of Natural History. "Numbers of Insects (Species and Individuals)," Aug. 2020.
https://www.si.edu/spotlight/buginfo/bugnos#:~:text=It%20has%20long%20been%20recognized,of%20living%20insects%20are%20known.

Department of Veterans Affairs. "Agent Orange Exposure and VA Disability Compensation," Sept.18, 2020,
https://www.va.gov/disability/eligibility/hazardous-materials-exposure/agent-orange/

Dickinson, Tim. "The True Cost of Carbon," by *Rolling Stone.* April 2020, https://www.rollingstone.com/culture/culture-features/how-to-reduce-carbon-emissions-971990/

Drake, Nadia. "Our Nights are Getting Brighter, and Earth Is Paying the Price," *National Geographic,* April 3, 2019,
https://www.nationalgeographic.com/science/2019/04/nights-are-getting-brighter-earth-paying-the-price-light-pollution-dark-skies/

Dybas, Cheryl and Wright, Matt. " New Study Finds World's Largest Desert, the Sahara, Has Grown By 10 Percent Since 1920," National Science Foundation, News Release 18-018, March 29, 2018,
https://www.nsf.gov/news/news_summ.jsp?cntn_id=244804

Egg, Jay. " 10 Myths About Geothermal Heating and Cooling," *National Geographic*,   Sept.17, 2013.
https://www.nationalgeographic.com/environment/great-energy-challenge/2013/10-myths-about-geothermal-heating-and-cooling/

Environmental Protection Agency, "Power Plant Emission Trends," Aug. 2020.   https://www.epa.gov/airmarkets/power-plant-emission-trends

Erickson, Britt E. "Neonicotinoid Pesticides Can Stay in the US Market, EPA Says," Feb. 3, 2020,
https://cen.acs.org/environment/pesticides/Neonicotinoid-pesticides-stay-US-market/98/web/2020/02#:~:text=The%20EPA%20advises%20homeowners%20not,their%20potential%20to%20harm%20bees.

Eschner, Kat. "Those Little Birds On The Backs Of Rhinos Actually Drink Blood," *Smithsonian Magazine*, Sept. 22, 2017, https://www.smithsonianmag.com/smart-news/those-little-birds-backs-rhinos-actually-drink-blood-180964912/

Evans Ogden, Lesley. "The Bittersweet Story of How We Stopped Acid Rain," BBC.com, Aug. 7, 2019,
https://www.bbc.com/future/article/20190823-can-lessons-from-acid-rain-help-stop-climate-change

Evers, Jeannie. and Caryl-Sue, "Great Pacific Garbage Patch," *National Geographic Society*, July 5, 2019,
https://www.nationalgeographic.org/encyclopedia/great-pacific-garbage-patch/

Fahrenkamp-Uppenbrink, Julia. " Wildflower Contamination with Neonicotinoids," *Science,* April 13, 2018,
https://science.sciencemag.org/content/360/6385/167.3#:~:text=Common%20blue%20butterfly%20larvae%20exposed,to%20harmful%20levels%20of%20neonicotinoids.

Fleshman, Michael. "Saving Africa's Forests, the 'Lungs of the World,' " *Africa Renewal Magazine*, Jan. 2008,
www.un.org/africarenewal/magazine/january-2008/saving-africa%E2%80%99s-forests-%E2%80%98lungs-world%E2%80%99

Forest Stewardship Council, https://fsc.org/en

Foster, Michael, et. al., "Increasing Neonicotinoid Use and the Declining Butterfly Fauna of Lowland California," royalsocietypublishing.org, August 1, 2016, https://royalsocietypublishing.org/doi/10.1098/rsbl.2016.0475

Fox, Douglas. "The Crisis in the Ice," *National Geographic,* July 2017, p. -----)

Furman, Dr. Tanya. and Guertin, Dr. Laura. "Lesson 6: The Nile River - Where Does The Water Go?," Penn State College of Earth and Mineral Sciences, July 2020. https://courseware.e-education.psu.edu/courses/earth105new/content/lesson06/04.html

Garson, Kelly. and Backstrom, Timothy. "European Union to Ban Chlorpyrifos after Jan. 31, 2020," Jan. 6, 2020, https://www.jdsupra.com/legalnews/european-union-to-ban-chlorpyrifos-54320/

Geophysical Fluid Dynamics Laboratory, NOAA. "Global Warming and Hurricanes," Sept. 18, 2020. https://www.gfdl.noaa.gov/global-warming-and-hurricanes/#global-warming-and-atlantic-hurricanes.

Gillam, Carey. "Dicamba Fact Sheet," US Right To Know, June 12, 2020, https://usrtk.org/pesticides/dicamba/

Goodell, Jeff. "Rising Tides, Troubled Waters," *Rolling Stone,* April 2020, p. 66.

Goodell, Jeffrey. "Rising Tides,Troubled Waters," by April 2020, *Rolling Stone.*

Green, Jenny. "Effects of Car Pollutants on the Environment," Sciencing.com, March 13, 2018, https://sciencing.com/effects-car-pollutants-environment-23581.html

Green, Miranda "Analysis: Trump Solar Tariffs Cost 62K US Jobs," *The Hill,* December 3, 2019, https://thehill.com/policy/energy-environment/472691-analysis-trump-solar-tariffs-cost-62k-us-jobs)

Gutiérrez Rodríguez, Lucas. Hogarth,Nicholas J. Zhou,Wen. Xie,Chen . Zhang,Kun. & Putzel, Louis. "China's Conversion of Cropland to Forest Program: a Systematic Review of the Environmental and Socioeconomic Effects," Environmental Evidence Journal, 21 (2016), Sept.12, 2016, https://environmentalevidencejournal.biomedcentral.com/articles/10.1186/s13750-016-0071-x#ref-CR10

Havard,Tiphanie. Laurent, Marion. Chauzat, Marie-Pierre. "Impact of Stressors on Honey Bees: Some Guidance for Research Emerge from a Meta-Analysis," www.ResearchGate.net , Dec. 20, 2019, https://www.researchgate.net/publication/338090539_Impact_of_Stressors_on_Honey_Bees_Apis_mellifera_Hymenoptera_Apidae_Some_Guidance_for_Research_Emerge_from_a_Meta-Analysis

Horn, Steve. "Arizona Reels as Three of the Biggest Wildfires in its History Ravage State," *The Guardian*, July 2, 2020, https://www.theguardian.com/environment/2020/jul/02/arizona-wildfires)

Horton, Jennifer. " How Ocean Currents Work," How Stuff Works, Aug. 2020, https://science.howstuffworks.com/environmental/earth/oceanography/ocean-current2.htm

Irfan, Umair. "Bitcoin is an Energy Hog. Where is all that Electricity Coming From?," Vox.com, June 18, 2019, https://www.vox.com/2019/6/18/18642645/bitcoin-energy-price-renewable-china

Jordan, Erin. "Eight Manure Lagoons Overflow in Western Iowa Because of Flooding," *Sioux City Journal,* March 26, 2019, https://siouxcityjournal.com/news/state-and-regional/iowa/eight-manure-lagoons-overflow-in-western-iowa-because-of-flooding/article_792b6561-c617-58ea-b287-70c58d3bb2bc.html)

Kane, Mouhamadou. "The Silent Destruction of Senegal's Last Forests," Jan. 10, 2019, https://enactafrica.org/enact-observer/the-silent-destruction-of-senegals-last-forests)

Knerl, Linsey. " What Every Gardener Should Know About Peat Moss (Plus 5 Alternatives)," *Gardeners Path*, July 25, 2017, https://gardenerspath.com/how-to/beginners/peat-moss/

Koenig, Ravena . "In Fairbanks, Building a Home on Permafrost Is Tricky," AP News, October 6, 2018, https://apnews.com/a3e0b1b176dc454b9cfb8fbc512219c9/In-Fairbanks,-building-a-home-on-permafrost-is-tricky#:~:text=Basically%2C%20Benesch's%20house%20is%20built,to%20water%20when%20it%20thaws.&text=That's%20a%20Fairbanks%2Dbased%20nonprofit,environments%20and%20provides%20public%20education.)

Kumar, Sanjay. "India Becomes World's Largest Emitter of Sulfur Dioxide," ChemistryWorld.com, Sept. 3, 2019, https://www.chemistryworld.com/news/india-becomes-worlds-largest-emitter-of-sulfur-dioxide/3010917.article)

Kurane, Ichiro . "The Effect of Global Warming on Infectious Diseases," National Center for Biotechnology Information, U.S. National Library of Medicine, Dec. 7, 2010, https://www.ncbi.nlm.nih.gov/pmc/articles/PMC3766891/#:~:text=Thus%2C%20the%20levels%20of%20the,%2C%20and%20tick%2Dborne%20encephalitis.

Lafond, Adrien. "What are the Main Sources of Nitrogen Oxides and Volatile Organic Compounds?" *Airboxlab US*, Sept. 2020, https://foobot.io/guides/what-are-the-main-sources-of-nitrogen-oxides-and-volatile-organic-compounds.php

Latham and Watkins, "US Fish and Wildlife Service Continues Work to Narrow Application of Migratory Bird Treaty Act," *Washington Post,* June 23, 2020, https://www.washingtonpost.com/news/energy-environment/wp/2018/04/13/the-trump-administration-officially-clipped-the-wings-of-the-migratory-bird-treaty-act/

Latif Dahir, Abdi. 'Like an Umbrella Had Covered the Sky': Locust Swarms Despoil Kenya," *The New York Times*, Feb. 21, 2020, https://www.nytimes.com/2020/02/21/world/africa/locusts-kenya-east-africa.html)

Law, Jessica. "Why We Need Birds (Far More Than They Need Us)," Jan. 4, 2019, https://www.birdlife.org/worldwide/news/why-we-need-birds-far-more-they-need-us

Leister, Eric and Pydynowski, Kristina. "Paris Breaks All-Time High Temperature As Deadly Heat Wave Shatters Records Across Europe," AccuWeather, July 25, 2019, https://www.accuweather.com/en/weather-news/paris-on-alert-for-record-breaking-temperatures-as-heat-wave-grips-spain-to-germany/461396.

Lila, Derick. "THE SAGA OF THE WHITE HOUSE SOLAR PANELS—A SOLAR STORY," June 5, 2017, https://pvbuzz.com/the-saga-of-the-white-house-solar-panels/#:~:text=The%20White%20House%20itself%20harvests,on%20the%20White%20House%20roof.&text=The%20White%20House%20did%20not%20have%20solar%20panels%20in%202000.

Lindsey, Rebecca. "Climate Change: Glacier Mass Balance," Climate.gov, *February 14, 2020,* https://www.climate.gov/news-features/understanding-climate/climate-change-glacier-mass-balance

Lindsey, Rebecca. "Climate Change: Glacier Mass Balance," Climate.gov, National Oceanic and Atmospheric Administration, Feb.14, 2020, https://www.climate.gov/news-features/understanding-climate/climate-change-glacier-mass-balance.

LokeshCBSE,"State the Role of Atmosphere in Climate Control," Discourse, CBSE Class 9, April 2019, https://ask.learncbse.in/t/state-the-role-of-atmosphere-in-climate-control/44018.

Loria, Kevin. "Miami Is Racing Against Time to Keep Up With Sea Level Rise," *Business Insider.* April 12, 2018, https://www.businessinsider.com/miami-floods-sea-level-rise-solutions-2018-4

Lovell, Daryl . "Agriculture Replaces Fossil Fuels as Largest Human Source of Sulfur to the Environment," University of Colorado Boulder, Aug.10, 2020, ttps://www.colorado.edu/today/2020/08/10/agriculture-replaces-fossil-fuels-largest-human-source-sulfur-environment

Mahr, Krista . "How Cape Town Was Saved From Running Out Of Water," *The Guardian*, May 4, 2018, https://www.theguardian.com/world/2018/may/04/back-from-the-brink-how-cape-town-cracked-its-water-crisis

Mahr, Krista. "How Cape Town Was Saved From Running Out Of Water," *The Guardian,* May 4, 2018, https://www.theguardian.com/world/2018/may/04/back-from-the-brink-how-cape-town-cracked-its-water-crisis

Marks, Andrea and Murphy, Hannah. "On the Eve of Extinction," *Rolling Stone,* April 2020, 1338.

Marlow, Iain and de Sousa, Agnieszka. "What It Will Take to Avoid a Global Food Shortage," Bloomburg.com, June 9, 2020, https://www.bloomberg.com/graphics/2020-solving-the-global-food-problem/

McGrath, Matt. "Nature Crisis: 'Insect Apocalypse' More Complicated thanThought," *BBC News*, April 23, 2020, https://www.bbc.com/news/science-environment-52399373#:~:text=Reports%20of%20the%20rapid%20and,caused%20great%20worry%20to%20scientists.&text=The%20compilation%20indicates%20that%20insects,lower%20than%20many%20published%20rates.)

Milman, Oliver. "US Glacier National Park Losing Its Glaciers With Just 26 of 150 Left," *The Guardian*, May 11, 2017, https://www.theguardian.com/environment/2017/may/11/us-glacier-national-park-is-losing-its-glaciers-with-just-26-of-150-left#:~:text=Some%20have%20lost%20as%20much,19th%20century%2C%20only%2026%20remain.

Muth, F. and Leonard, A.S. " A Neonicotinoid Pesticide Impairs Foraging, But Not Learning, in Free-Flying Bumblebees," *Scientific Reports*, Nature Research, 2019, https://www.nature.com/articles/s41598-019-39701-5

NASA Climate Kids. "What Is Permafrost?" Aug. 2020, https://climatekids.nasa.gov/permafrost/#:~:text=and%20South%20Poles.-,Permafrost%20is%20any%20ground%20that%20remains%20completely%20frozen%E2%80%9432%C2%B0,large%20regions%20of%20the%20Earth.

National Museum of Natural History. "Extinction of Plants and Animals," Smithsonian Institution, https://naturalhistory.si.edu/education/teaching-resources/paleontology/extinction-over-time

National Ocean Service, "The Importance of Coral Reefs," June 2020, https://oceanservice.noaa.gov/education/tutorial_corals/coral07_importance.html

National Ocean Service. "Anthropogenic (Human) Threats to Corals," May 2020, https://oceanservice.noaa.gov/education/tutorial_corals/coral09_humanthreats.html

National Oceanic and Atmospheric Administration. "Ocean Acidification," April 2020, https://www.noaa.gov/education/resource-collections/ocean-coasts/ocean-acidification#:~:text=Because%20of%20human%2Ddriven%20increased,the%20ocean%20becomes%20more%20acidic.)

Nelson, Angela. "7 Surprising Health Benefits of Mushrooms," Treehugger.com, January 22, 2020, https://www.treehugger.com/surprising-health-benefits-mushrooms-4864212)

Nissenbaum, Dion and Osseiran, Nazih. "A Row Over Trees Could Spark the Next Israel-Lebanon War," *The Wall Street Journal*, June 28, 2020, https://www.wsj.com/articles/a-row-over-trees-could-spark-the-next-israel-lebanon-war-11593345635

Nunez, Christina. "Acid Rain Explained," *National Geographic,* Feb. 28, 2019, https://www.nationalgeographic.com/environment/global-warming/acid-rain/

Paddock, Richard C. "Indonesia Lets Plastic Burning Continue Despite Warning on Toxins," *The New York Times*, Dec. 19, 2019. https://www.nytimes.com/2019/12/19/world/asia/indonesia-dioxin-plastic-tofu.html)

Pala, Christopher. "Kiribati's President's Plans to Raise Islands in Fight Against Sea-Level Rise," *The Guardian*, Aug. 9, 2020, https://www.theguardian.com/world/2020/aug/10/kiribatis-presidents-plans-to-raise-islands-in-fight-against-sea-level-rise

Pallardy, Richard. "Deepwater Horizon Oil Spill," Britannica.com, April 13, 2020, https://www.britannica.com/event/Deepwater-Horizon-oil-spill

Papiewski, John. "What Kind of Light Does a Solar Cell Need?," March 10, 2018, https://sciencing.com/kind-light-solar-cell-need-21539.html

Pennsylvania Department of Agriculture. "Spotted Lanternfly Alert," PA, 2019. https://www.agriculture.pa.gov/Plants_Land_Water/PlantIndustry/Entomology/spotted_lanternfly/SpottedLanternflyAlert/Pages/default.aspx

Perkins, Lori . "Global Temperature Anomalies from 1880 to 2019," *Scientific Visualization Studio*, NASA, Jan.15, 2020, https://svs.gsfc.nasa.gov/4787.

Petrescu, Florian Ion. "Nuclear Fusion," Bucharest Polytechnic University, July 31, 2012, https://www.altenergymag.com/article/2012/07/nuclear-fusion/1090#:~:text=Raw%20materials%20for%20fusion%20are,far%20superior%20to%20nuclear%20fission.

Petts, James. "2020 is the First Bonn Challenge Deadline. What Does the Barometer Say?," Sept. 1, 2020, https://news.globallandscapesforum.org/38040/2020-is-the-first-bonn-challenge-deadline-what-does-the-barometer-say/

Pierre-Louis, Kendra. "Lagoons of Pig Waste Are Overflowing After Florence. Yes, That's as Nasty as It Sounds." *The New York Times,* Sept. 19, 2018, https://www.nytimes.com/2018/09/19/climate/florence-hog-farms.html

Platt, John R. "The Faces of Extinction: The Species We Lost in 2019," Jan. 6, 2020, https://therevelator.org/extinction-species-lost-2019/

Ponder,Lance. "Fossil Fuel," Bible.org, August 29, 2011, https://bible.org/seriespage/18-fossil-fuel

Ritchie, Hannah. And Roser, Max. "Fossil Fuels," OurWorldinData.org, Aug. 2020.https://ourworldindata.org/fossil-fuels

Robinson, Mary. Climate Justice (Berryville, VA: Berryville Graphics, Inc., 2018).

Roos, Sandin, Zamani and Peters, "REPORT: Environmental Assessment of Swedish Fashion Consumption," MistraFutureFashion.com, June 15, 2015, http://mistrafuturefashion.com/wp-content/uploads/2015/06/Environmental-assessment-of-Swedish-fashion-consumption-LCA.pdf

Sabate, J., et al, "The Environmental Cost of Protein Food Choices," *Cambridge Core,* Cambridge.org, Aug. 2015. https://www.cambridge.org/core/journals/public-health-nutrition/article/environmental-cost-of-protein-food-choices/DB40E5C12D662913CC342D3C19F85F7D/core-reader#

Schwartz, John. " Plastic? It's Everywhere, Even in the Air We Breathe, Scientists Report," *The New York Times*, June 12, 2020.

Schwartz, Judith. "Soil as Carbon Storehouse: New Weapon in Climate Fight?" Yale University, March 4, 2014, https://e360.yale.edu/features/soil_as_carbon_storehouse_new_weapon_in_climate_fight

Semuels, Alana. "Is This the End of Recycling?," *The Atlantic,* March 5, 2019, https://www.theatlantic.com/technology/archive/2019/03/china-has-stopped-accepting-our-trash/584131/

Shahbandeh, M. "Top 10 U.S. states by inventory of hogs and pigs as of March 2020 (in 1,000s)," April 30, 2020, https://www.statista.com/statistics/194371/top-10-us-states-by-number-of-hogs-and-pigs/

Shortridge, Robert W. "Some Early History of Hydroelectric Power," www.hydroreview.com, June 1988. http://www.hydroreview.com/wp-content/uploads/content/dam/hydro/Document/earlyhistoryrev2.pdf

Skene, Jennifer. "The Issue With the Tissue," National Resource Defense Council, Feb. 2019, https://www.nrdc.org/sites/default/files/issue-tissue-how-americans-are-flushing-forests-down-toilet-report.pdf

Skene, Jennifer. "THE ISSUE WITH TISSUE: HOW AMERICANS ARE FLUSHING FORESTS DOWN THE TOILET," Feb. 2019, https://www.nrdc.org/sites/default/files/issue-tissue-how-americans-are-flushing-forests-down-toilet-report.pdf

Snelling, Dr. Andrew, "Coal Beds and Noah's Flood," Answers in Genesis.org, June 1, 1986, https://answersingenesis.org/geology/catastrophism/coal-beds-and-noahs-flood/).

Society for Experimental Biology. "Lights Out: Light Pollution Alters Reproduction Cycle in Lemurs," *Science Daily*, July 2, 2014, www.sciencedaily.com/releases/2014/07/140702203804.htm

Stibich, Mark,PhD. "The Best Types of Fish to Avoid Mercury," *Very Well Fit,* April 13, 2020,
          https://www.verywellfit.com/the-best-types-of-fish-for-health-2223830.
Sullivan, Brian. "World's Oceans Now Warmest on Record, Increasing Risk of Hurricanes, Wildfires," *Time,* April 20,
          2020, https://time.com/5824299/ocean-temperature-rise-climate-change/
Sullivan, Laura. "How Big Oil Misled The Public Into Believing Plastic Would Be Recycled," *National Public Radio*, Sept.
          11,2020, https://www.npr.org/2020/09/11/897692090/how-big-oil-misled-the-public-into-believing-plastic-
          would-be-recycled
Taylor, Derrick Bryson. "Antarctica Sets Record High Temperature: 64.9 Degrees," *New York Times*, Feb. 8, 2020,
          https://www.nytimes.com/2020/02/08/climate/antarctica-record-temperature.html.
the environmentor, "Fact Check: Are There Really More Trees Today Than 100 Years Ago?", tentree.com, Oct.22,
          2017, https://www.tentree.com/blogs/posts/fact-check-are-there-really-more-trees-today-than-100-years-
          ago#:~:text=We%20had%20rudimentary%20estimates%20based,good%20or%20well%2Ddocumented%20s
          cience.
Thompson, "The Aral Sea Crisis," Columbia.edu, July, 2020,
          http://www.columbia.edu/~tmt2120/environmental%20impacts.htm)
Tiassou, Kossivi. "Amazon versus Africa forest fires: Is the world really ablaze?". *Deustche Well*e, July 2020,
          (https://www.dw.com/en/amazon-versus-africa-forest-fires-is-the-world-really-ablaze/a-50229553
Township of Stafford, NJ. "130-52 Selective Clearing," June 2020,   https://ecode360.com/11376158
Trenchard, Tommy. " 'There's No More Water': Climate Change on a Drying Island," *New York Times*, April 16, 2020,
          https://www.nytimes.com/2020/04/16/world/africa/comoros-climate-change-rivers.html)
United Nations Convention to Combat Desertification. "The Great Green Wall Initiative," Sept. 2020,
          https://www.unccd.int/actions/great-green-wall-initiative
United Nations Economic Commission for Europe. "Air Pollution and Health," Aug. 2020,
          https://www.unece.org/environmental-policy/conventions/envlrtapwelcome/cross-sectoral-linkages/air-
          pollution-and-health.html
United Nations Environment Assembly. "Tackling global water pollution," Sept. 2020,
          https://www.unenvironment.org/explore-topics/water/what-we-do/tackling-global-water-pollution)
United States Environmental Protection Agency. "Why is Acid Rain Harmful?," July 2020.
          https://www3.epa.gov/acidrain/education/site_students/whyharmful.html#:~:text=Acid%20Rain%20Harms%20
          Forests&text=Acid%20rain%20that%20seeps%20into,trees%20to%20take%20up%20water.
University of Wisconsin - Madison, "What Determines Sky's Colors At Sunrise And Sunset?," *ScienceDaily,* Nov. 15,
          2007,
          https://www.sciencedaily.com/releases/2007/11/071108135522.htm#:~:text=Summary%3A,rays%2C%20cau
          sing%20them%20to%20scatter.
Unwin, Jack. "What is Geothermal Energy?," Power-technology.com, June 18, 2019,   https://www.power-
          technology.com/features/what-is-geothermal-energy/
US Environmental Protection Agency, "Climate Change Indicators: Atmospheric Concentrations of Greenhouse
          Gases," April 2016.   https://www.epa.gov/climate-indicators/climate-change-indicators-atmospheric-
          concentrations-greenhouse-gases.
US Environmental Protection Agency. "Mercury Emissions: The Global Context," Jan. 28, 2020,
          https://www.epa.gov/international-cooperation/mercury-emissions-global-
          context#:~:text=Mercury%20occurs%20naturally%20in%20the,can%20be%20washed%20into%20water.)
US Geological Survey, "25 Years After the Exxon Valdez, Sea Otter Population at Pre-Spill Levels," Feb. 28, 2014,
          https://www.usgs.gov/news/25-years-after-exxon-valdez-sea-otter-population-pre-spill-levels
Walsh, Declan. and Sengupta, Somini .   "For Thousands of Years, Egypt Controlled the Nile. A New Dam Threatens
          That," *The New York Times*, Feb. 9, 2020, ttps://www.nytimes.com/interactive/2020/02/09/world/africa/nile-
          river-dam.html
Welch, Craig. "Why Cape Town Is Running Out Of Water and Who Is Next?" *National Geographic,* March 5, 2018,
          https://www.nationalgeographic.com/news/2018/02/cape-town-running-out-of-water-drought-taps-shutoff-
          other-cities/
Wheeling, K. "Toxic Algal Blooms Are Worsening with Climate Change," Eos.org. Nov.13, 2019,
          https://eos.org/articles/toxic-algal-blooms-are-worsening-with-climate-change
World Health Organization. "Zoonoses," July 29, 2020,   https://www.who.int/news-room/fact-sheets/detail/zoonoses
Wynes, Seth. and Nicholas, Kimberly A. "2017 Environmental Research Letters," in Dickinson, Tim. "The True Cost of
          Carbon," *Rolling Stone*, April 2020, https://www.rollingstone.com/culture/culture-features/how-to-reduce-
          carbon-emissions-971990/
Yeung, Jessie . "A Blob of Hot Water in the Pacific Ocean Killed a Million Seabirds, Scientists Say," *CNN World*,
          Jan.16, 2020, https://www.cnn.com/2020/01/16/world/blob-seabird-study-intl-hnk-scli-scn/index.html)

Zhang, Qi, et al., "Divergent socioeconomic-ecological outcomes of China's conversion of cropland to forest program in the subtropical mountainous area and the semi-arid Loess Plateau," *Science Direct,* October 2020, https://www.sciencedirect.com/science/article/pii/S2212041620301091#s0050

" List of Crop Plants Pollinated by Bees," *Wikipedia.* June 2020, https://en.wikipedia.org/wiki/List_of_crop_plants_pollinated_by_bees

"Agricultural Land Use Decouples Soil Nutrient Cycles in a Subtropical Riparian Wetland in China," CATENA, *ScienceDirect,* October 2015,, https://www.sciencedirect.com/science/article/abs/pii/S0341816215300114

"Air Pollution:How We Are Changing the Air," University Corporation for Atmospheric Research, Center for Science Education, 2020, https://scied.ucar.edu/learning-zone/air-quality/air-pollution

"Amazon Fires at 13-Year High for June," The Visual and Data Journalism Team. BBC News, July 2, 2020, https://www.bbc.com/news/world-latin-america-49433767)

"Atmosphere, Composition and Structure," Encyclopedia.com, Aug. 22, 2020, https://www.encyclopedia.com/science/encyclopedias-almanacs-transcripts-and-maps/atmosphere-composition-and-structure.

"Basics of Wind Energy," *American Wind Energy Association.* Aug. 2020, https://www.awea.org/wind-101/basics-of-wind-energy

"Browse 41,997 CITIES WORLDWIDE," Sept. 2020, https://www.weatherbase.com/

"Chlorofluorocarbon, " *Wikipedia*, Sept. 2020, https://en.wikipedia.org/wiki/Chlorofluorocarbon#:~:text=Since%20the%20late%201970s%2C%20the,effects%20on%20the%20ozone%20layer.&text=In%201978%2C%20under%20the%20Toxic,of%20CFCS%20and%20aerosol%20propellants.)

"Chlorpyrifos, Compound Summary". National Library of Medicine, June 2020, https://pubchem.ncbi.nlm.nih.gov/compound/Chlorpyrifos

"Chlorpyrifos," *Wikipedia*. June 2020, https://en.wikipedia.org/wiki/Chlorpyrifos

"Environmental Impact of Toilet Paper," The World Counts, June 2020, https://www.theworldcounts.com/challenges/consumption/other-products/environmental-impact-of-toilet-paper/story

"Environmental Impacts of Natural Gas," the Union of Concerned Scientists, June 19, 2014, https://www.ucsusa.org/resources/environmental-impacts-natural-gas#:~:text=Air%20pollution,sulfur%2C%20mercury%2C%20and%20particulates.&text=Exposure%20to%20elevated%20levels%20of,%2C%20and%20cancer%20%5B11%5D.

"Environmental Problems with Fertilizers," Argo Services International, Aug. 2020, https://www.agroservicesinternational.com/Environment/Problems.html#:~:text=Problems%20with%20fertilizers,water%20with%20nitrates%20and%20phosphates.&text=These%20algae%20eventually%20die%20and,This%20process%20is%20called%20eutrophication.

"Food Choices and the Planet," Earthsave.org, July 2020, https://www.earthsave.org/environment.htm

"Global Forest Watch - Fires," globalforestwatch.org, July 2020, https://fires.globalforestwatch.org/report/index.html#aoitype=ALL&reporttype=globalcountryreport&dates=fYear-2019!fMonth-7!fDay-7!tYear-2020!tMonth-7!tDay-6)

"History of Solar Energy: Who Invented Solar Panels?," Vinint.Solar, www.vinitsolar.com , Aug. 2020. https://www.vivintsolar.com/learning-center/history-of-solar-energy

"History: Early Wind Power," Thirdplanetwind.com. July 2020, http://www.thirdplanetwind.com/energy/history.aspx#:~:text=The%20earliest%20known%20wind%20powered,in%20his%20Connecticut%20machine%20shop.

"How Do You Gather and Harvest Natural Gas?" KB Delta Compressor Valve Parts, KBDelta.com. July 2020. https://kbdelta.com/blog/gather-harvest-natural-gas.html#:~:text=The%20easiest%20way%20to%20access,are%20referred%20to%20as%20wells.

"How Energy Storage Works," The Union of Concerned Scientists, www.ucsusa.org , Feb. 19, 2015, https://www.ucsusa.org/resources/how-energy-storage-works#:~:text=Many%20hydroelectric%20power%20plants%20include,through%20turbines%20to%20generate%20electricity.

"Imidacloprid," *Wikipedia.* May 2019, https://en.wikipedia.org/wiki/Imidacloprid#Bees_and_other_insects

"India - Nitrous Oxide Emissions," Knoema.com, July 2020, https://knoema.com/atlas/India/topics/Environment/Emissions/Nitrous-oxide-emissions#:~:text=In%202012%2C%20nitrous%20oxide%20emissions,average%20annual%20rate%20of%201.42%25.

"Marine Mammals and Sonar," *Wikipedia.* March 25, 2020, https://en.wikipedia.org/wiki/Marine_mammals_and_sonar#Scientific_attention

"Meat Eaters Guide Report: Climate and Environmental Impacts, 2011," Environmental Working Group,
https://www.ewg.org/meateatersguide/a-meat-eaters-guide-to-climate-change-health-what-you-eat-matters/climate-and-environmental-impacts/

"Million Trees Project," Livinglandsandwaters.org, https://www.livinglandsandwaters.org/what-we-do/our-projects/milliontrees-project.html)

"Myth: Roundup is safe herbicide with low toxicity to animals and humans," GMO Myths and Truths, Earthopensource.org, Sept. 2020, https://earthopensource.org/gmomythsandtruths/sample-page/4-health-hazards-roundup-glyphosate/4-1-myth-roundup-safe-herbicide-low-toxicity-animals-humans/#:~:text=Glyphosate%20and%20its%20main%20metabolite,and%20in%20mice%20in%20vivo.&text=Such%20damage%20to%20DNA%20may,of%20cancer%20and%20birth%20defects.

"Nuclear Energy, Environmental Impact," *Wikipedia*. June 2020,
https://en.wikipedia.org/wiki/Nuclear_power#Environmental_impact

"People and Frozen Ground," National Snow and Ice Data Center, University of Colorado Boulder, July 2020.
https://nsidc.org/cryosphere/frozenground/people.html

"Plastics Pollution," Conference Series, Aug. 2020, https://pollution.conferenceseries.com/events-list/plastic-pollution

"Pollution Impacts," *World Wildlife*. Aug. 2020, https://www.worldwildlife.org/threats/pollution

"Restore Our Future: The Bonn Challenge, " International Union for Conservation of Nature, June 2020,
https://www.bonnchallenge.org/content/challenge

"Rosy Periwinkle," The Living Rain Forest. May 2020, https://livingrainforest.org/learning-resources/rosy-periwinkle

"Spruce Budworm," *Wikipedia*. June 2020, https://en.wikipedia.org/wiki/Spruce_budworm

"State by State Information," American Coalition of Competitive Energy Suppliers, July 2020,
http://competitiveenergy.org/consumer-tools/state-by-state-links/#:~:text=New%20Jersey,and%20Rockland%20Electric%20utility%20territories.

"Tailings - Environmental Considerations and Case Studies," *Wikipedia*. Aug. 2020,
https://en.wikipedia.org/wiki/Tailings#Environmental_considerations_and_case_studies)

"The Amazon in Brazil is on Fire - How Bad is it?" The Visual and Data Journalism Team. *BBC News*.
https://www.bbc.com/news/world-latin-america-49433767

"The Halliburton Loophole," Earthworks.org, June 2020,
tps://earthworks.org/issues/inadequate_regulation_of_hydraulic_fracturing/

"The Truth About Recycling." 5 Gyres Science to Solutions, 5Gyres.org, Sept. 2020, https://www.5gyres.org/truth-about-recycling

"Top 10 Medicinal Plants of the Amazon," RainforestsCruises.com, Feb.17, 2016,
https://www.rainforestcruises.com/jungle-blog/top-10-medicinal-plants-of-the-amazon

"U.S. ENERGY SYSTEM FACTSHEET," Center for Sustainable Systems, University of Michigan, 2020,
http://css.umich.edu/factsheets/us-energy-system-factsheet

"Viniculture: European Scale," Climate Change Post. Center for Climate Adaptation.
https://www.climatechangepost.com/europe/viniculture/

"What Are PFOAs And PFOs And How Dangerous Are They?," The Environmental Pollution Centers, Feb. 21, 2018,
https://www.environmentalpollutioncenters.org/news/what-are-pfoa-and-pfos-and-how-dangerous-are-they/

"What Happened to Africa's Ambitious Green Belt Project?" *Deutsche Welle*, Aug. 2020, https://www.dw.com/en/what-happened-to-africas-ambitious-green-belt-project/a-53004690

"What Is Noise Pollution?" The Environmental Pollution Center, 2017,
https://www.environmentalpollutioncenters.org/noise-pollution/#:~:text=Noise%20pollution%20is%20generally%20defined,or%20consistent%20the%20exposure%20is.

"What is Sustainable Agriculture?" Union of Concerned Scientists, Apr. 10, 2017,
https://www.ucsusa.org/resources/what-sustainable-agriculture

"World Animal Day: We Honour Elephant & Rhino," Kariega Game Reserve. Oct. 4, 2019,
https://www.kariega.co.za/blog/world-animal-day-we-honour-elephant-rhino